10/10

D0359994

WITHDRAWN

2017 ✓

FRIENDSHIP
for GROWN-UPS

Also by Lisa Whelchel

FRIENDSHIP
for GROWN-UPS

What I Missed and
Learned Along the Way

LISA WHELCHEL

THOMAS NELSON
Since 1798

NASHVILLE   DALLAS   MEXICO CITY   RIO DE JANEIRO

Published in Nashville, Tennessee, by Thomas Nelson. Thomas Nelson is a registered trademark of Thomas Nelson, Inc.

Thomas Nelson, Inc., titles may be purchased in bulk for educational, business, fund-raising, or sales promotional use. For information, please e-mail SpecialMarkets@ThomasNelson.com.

Library of Congress Cataloging-in-Publication Data

Whelchel, Lisa.
  Friendship for grown-ups : what I missed and learned along the way / Lisa Whelchel.
    p. cm.
  ISBN 978-1-4002-0277-5
  1. Christian women—Religious life. 2. Female friendship—Religious aspects—Christianity. I. Title.
  BV4527.W457 2010
  241'.6762082—dc22

2010002949

Printed in the United States of America

10 11 12 13 14 WCF 6 5 4 3 2 1

FOR NEY BAILEY,
*who is grace incarnate, wisdom revealed, love displayed,
mercy manifest, tenderness personified,
friendship exemplified.*

Thank God for this gift too wonderful for words.
—2 CORINTHIANS 9:15 (NLT)

Contents

CONTENTS

Foreword

My Dear Friend, Lisa

I vividly remember the first time Lisa and I met. She was carrying a pink box of donuts into a Sunday school class of lively five-year-olds. "Teacher Lisa" was supposed to help my husband and me learn how to keep another group of munchkins busy for an hour and a half, since we were signed up to teach our own class the following month.

Lisa was very friendly, funny, and fun to watch in action. I liked her immediately but knew there was no chance to really get to know her since she probably had a million people in her life and was busy being a celebrity and all. So I gave her space.

Then Lisa and I were pregnant at the same time with our firstborn children. We instantly had a lot in common and began chatting more. Lisa and her husband, Steve, an associate pastor at our church, invited a small group of us from church over for dinner one night—probably, I assumed, to do the pastoral thing of reaching out to members of the congregation.

We had a great time, but I noticed that Lisa always shifted the conversation away from anything about her. I was really interested to learn about her life, as I would be any new friend, but there was an immediate drop of the curtain whenever I asked questions about Lisa's thoughts or experiences. The message was clear: getting too personal was off-limits. I drew the conclusion that celebrities cannot afford to let their guard down because they never know who's trying to get close to them just because of status.

Once again I backed off and gave space to Lisa.

Then, having our babies at the same time, taking parenting classes together, pulling out our hair trying to raise smart and well-adjusted kids, homeschooling, and taking several vacations together, I could finally call Lisa my friend. I absolutely loved spending time with her. She was so creative, insightful, and fun. And yet, sadly, I knew that our friendship probably would never go beyond a certain level. Lisa didn't show emotion or weakness, so how could I let myself be vulnerable with her? She had that inner strength that made her a super-duper-power-Christian and left me a struggling-wannabe.

Unfortunately there came a horrific point in my life

when I had a total emotional and physical breakdown. During those awful months, Lisa came alongside and did not hesitate to take over the homeschooling of my two oldest children, even though she was already homeschooling her own three children. Lisa showed me honest compassion and offered me the physical help that I couldn't have survived without. I never got the feeling that she was doing this out of obligation—but instead out of genuine love and concern. My kids still look back on that year as one of their all-time favorites.

Even after all of that, I still didn't feel that I could completely be myself with Lisa because I never felt that she could be completely honest with me. From time to time, she would bring down her wall a few bricks for me to see the gold mine on the other side, but she was always quick to rebuild that wall whenever she began to feel vulnerable or uncomfortable.

At the same time, I was always so amazed at how Lisa handled everything. She was a spiritual rock. All she needed to get through the difficult times in her life was to lean on God and trust that, as Paul writes in Romans 8:28, "in all things God works for the good of those who love him." It was so simple, but it was so not my own life experience. I really couldn't talk much to her about my pain, and she, of course, didn't show that she had any of her own. We loved each other dearly, but once again, there was only so far our friendship could go.

A few years ago there was a dramatic shift in Lisa. I saw her cry for the first time—ever. She began to be really honest, and I mean really honest. She was dealing with deep heartbreak that shined a spotlight on the pain she had so carefully kept tucked away her whole life in order to keep functioning as a wife and mother. Suddenly, though, Lisa's way of coping with life, by living in partial denial, wasn't working anymore. She became vulnerable and open and to talk with her was like talking to a completely different person.

This is when Lisa and I began to share deeply, cry together, and openly express anger, frustration, and hurt. She wasn't the perfect power Christian anymore. She finally was someone with whom I could relate. I began to feel like we were in this struggle of life together, complete with all the joys and anguish that go with it. There weren't any more pat answers, just genuine love and support.

For the first time, Lisa began to trust me. It took sixteen years, but it was well worth the wait.

Today Lisa is one of my most precious friends. She was one of the first people I e-mailed this year when a close friend of mine died and when I got some scary medical news. In each instance, she responded in ways that made me feel completely loved and supported.

Because she has chosen to do the hard thing and work through her own pain, Lisa knows how to love and comfort others. Doing the hard thing, of course, means Lisa is on a journey that is both terrifying and right. Letting go of denial and choosing to live life fully, open and vulnerable, is one of the most challenging things a person can do. Making that shift requires falling—and being willing to fall takes spectacular courage. I've witnessed both things in Lisa and, ultimately, how they are making her the beautiful, trusted friend I have today. I admire her in her professional life, in her family life, and especially in her determination to heal from the inside out. She has gone from a distant but fun person to a dear friend with whom I can pour out my heart.

And the really cool thing? We still know how to simply laugh together.

Janice Clark
wife, mother, personal trainer, friend

Acknowledgments

So Grateful

This is my most and least favorite part of writing a book. I love, love, love the opportunity to tell the world how grateful I am for the people in my life who have walked this particular journey with me. The problem is, words are so very inadequate to express the depth of my appreciation. So, if you could, please read each acknowledgment as if the words were in a bold, underlined, 72-point type. Then, grab a thesaurus and apply every nuance, texture, and amplification of meaning. Put on a moving piece of music, gaze at a timeless work of art, or read this page on the beach at sunset. Perhaps then you will comprehend a glimmer of my gratitude.

My beloved family: Steve, Tucker, Haven, and Clancy: you are my white space to the written word, my rests in a symphony, and light within a painting. Without you, my life and ministry would be a confusing cacophony of foggy meaning.

My first best friend, my mom; and three generations of mothers, daughters, granddaughters, and girlfriends: it's said that "blood is thicker than water." I don't know who said that first, but he or she must have had a family bond like we do. *Thank you* seems trite in the face of a lifetime of love.

The Women of Faith Porch and Back Porch: just as a porch is attached to a house, you are deeply connected to the home of my heart. With you, I enjoy meandering conversations, wordless understanding, delicious conviviality, and challenging grace.

Michael Hyatt, Bryan Norman, and Thomas Nelson Publishers: oddly enough, I know you on a personal level even more than a professional level (thank you, Twitter). I can truly say how much I respect and like you. May our friendships extend beyond even the best of business relationships.

Jennifer, Priscilla, Angela, Michele, Amy, Good Medicine Club, MomTime, and LifeNet friends: you know that I would love to mention you all by name and proclaim from the mountaintops how each one of you has impacted and continues to impact my life. Just know I am envisioning your faces individually, and my soul is smiling at the thought of you.

ACKNOWLEDGMENTS

My great cloud of influences: Henry Cloud, Sarah Young, Richard Rohr, Gerald May, Brennan Manning, Wayne Jacobsen, Henri Nouwen, John Eldredge, Eugene Peterson, Richard Foster, John Townsend, Timothy Keller, Walter Wangerin, Frederick Buechner, Charles Swindoll, Larry Crabb, Dan Allender, and Francine Rivers. Although I don't know you personally, I have been profoundly changed by your writings. Heaven will be heaven to me because I will get to talk to you as long as I want, ask you every question I have ever wondered, and thank you in person.

One

I Need Friends

few years ago, I was asked to film *The Facts of Life* reunion movie and was thrilled. I still love all my friends from the show and am often asked about them.

In fact, one of the first questions I am always asked when someone recognizes me is, "Do you still keep in touch with the girls from the show?"

The answer is, "Yes, we do. But we don't see each other often." The situation is probably the same as with your girlfriends from high school and college. You are so close and you think you'll never grow apart, but life marches on and you find yourself heading down diverging paths. Whenever you get back together, though, things seem just like old times.

That's the best way to describe my relationship with the girls on the show, and that is exactly how it felt on the first day of rehearsal for the television reunion movie. The only difference was, instead of us being four girls over in the corner giggling between filming takes, we were grown women giggling in the corner.

One other thing hadn't changed. Have you ever noticed how junior high girls sometimes bond with each other by talking about another girl behind her back? It isn't that they don't like the other girl. Sometimes it's simply that they are bonding with this particular friend at the moment.

Have you also ever noticed that, even after we grow up, we sometimes still act like little girls, especially when we get together with friends? Well, this is what happened on the very first day of rehearsal for the telepic. All of us girls fell right back into sophomoric behavior by forming little cliques and talking about whoever wasn't in the room at the time.

For instance, Kim Fields (who played Tootie) and I would huddle in the corner and I might say, "Oh my goodness, can you believe Mindy did _____" (fill in the blank). Later, I'd be with Mindy (Cohn, who played Natalie) and say, "Well, I don't want to judge, but I heard that Kim . . ." But I didn't stop there. Oh no, I had to take it one step further.

When I got back to the hotel room that night, I called Nancy McKeon (who played Jo) back home in California.

Nancy was filming a television series and wasn't able to be in the reunion movie. When she answered the phone, I blurted, "We miss you terribly. Blair is only half the fun without Jo!" Then I jumped right in, "You are not going to believe Kim did this and Mindy said that and on and on." By the end of the conversation, we had had a positive bonding experience by talking negatively about the other girls.

I went to bed that evening but woke up in the night and couldn't get back to sleep. Out of the quiet, I heard the Lord whisper to my heart: *You know, Lisa, you don't know why Kim does what you were gossiping about, and you don't have a clue about what Mindy is going through. But I know. And I would appreciate it if you wouldn't talk about my little girls that way.*

I felt terrible. I love Kim, Mindy, and Nancy very much. I didn't mean anything bad by the things we were talking about. The truth is that all the talk I was making about them really was more about me—I was feeling extremely insecure that first day of rehearsal. It had been fifteen years since I had done any acting, and I felt so out of shape.

"I feel like a baseball player must feel after not playing in years," I had told my husband that night. "The timing of my swing is off, my throwing arm is weak. I'm striking out and overthrowing first base. I wonder if I still have what it takes?"

Because so much of my identity has been intertwined

with performance, I was scared—and out of that fear I was attacking others. I wasn't being a safe person.

Thankfully, in the dark of the night, God brought my issue to light where healing could happen. As I realized my wrongs, I determined to set things right. The first thing I did was call Nancy and confess that I shouldn't have talked about our friends behind their backs. I even apologized for saying some things about her. Thankfully, she wasn't at home, so I only had to leave a message on her voice mail.

For the rest of the month of filming, I was careful to speak only positive things. If someone came up to me and started talking about someone else, I would say, "You know, I've noticed that she does that, but have you seen how much she's grown in other areas?" Or someone might start a conversation with me like, "I can't believe so-and-so would do such-and-such," to which I would reply, "I can't believe it either. I find myself doing the same thing sometimes. I wonder if we'll ever grow up!"

An interesting thing happened. I was soon perceived as a safe person. Over the weeks the cast and crew drew close to me, and we had wonderful conversations and times of bonding. At the end of the month, on the last day of filming, so many people came up to me and said: "Lisa, when you arrive on the set, it is like a rainbow appears." "You just don't carry any baggage with you to work, do you?" "I've been watching you this month. You're different."

Yes, there is a time and place for healing words. What

I didn't know until this experience was that sometimes more healing is available to others by the things we don't say than by the things we do say. People are hungry for safe havens. Places where they can be themselves—without judgment, fear of exposure, or betrayal. People hunger for spaces of grace, understanding, acceptance. Safe people know what God was trying to tell me in the middle of the night. Despite what we think we see on the outside, everyone is hurting on the inside. If we have allowed God to come inside our hurting places to bring love and healing, then even if we haven't walked in their shoes to know what they're going through, we can know what it feels like to be hurt and healed.

Early Lessons

I wish I could report that I continued to steadily grow in the area of friendships after this lesson, but unfortunately, that isn't the case. My history with friendships has been sputtering, at best. I left home when I was twelve to move to Hollywood and was working in television during most of my school-age years when we typically learn the ins and outs of friendship. And my experiences before that weren't all that positive.

I was painfully shy, which is the reason I got into acting in the first place. My second-grade teacher, Mrs. Clark, was worried because I rarely went out on the playground at recess. I preferred to sit on the sidelines and read a book or, better yet, stay in the room and help her.

During a parent-teacher meeting, she shared her concerns with my mother, who then signed me up for a drama class to help me overcome my shyness. It worked as long as I was performing on stage, but I was still a scared little mouse one-on-one.

My best friend from third grade on was a preacher's kid named Paul. He grew up to be the valedictorian of the senior class and now lives in Greenwich Village as an opera singer. I was considered a Jesus Freak who wore a huge wooden cross necklace and carried my Bible to school to have Bible study with Paul at lunch. We were quite a pair. As you can imagine, we weren't part of the popular crowd.

Oh, I had friends on my softball team and in my Girl Scout troop, but I always felt like an outsider. It wasn't just my imagination. I did march to the beat of a different drummer—which has the same effect on "mean girls" as the scent of blood has on sharks. I remember changing classes one day in sixth grade. Just the weekend before, I had won a citywide talent show as a ventriloquist, and my picture was in the local paper. A handful of girls brought the newspaper to school and cornered me in the hall. They surrounded me, and at first, I thought they were sincerely proud of me.

I was wrong. With smiles on their faces, the girls held the paper in front of my nose and tore it down the middle.

Perhaps it was a mercy that I didn't have a traditional junior high or high school experience.

But I missed that whole time period when it's relatively safe to learn from your mistakes; navigating the world of close friendships for the first time in my forties has been awkward, to say the least.

On the upside, I am older and wiser now, enough to observe myself go through it while at the same time experiencing it. That means I can learn from my friendship foibles and faux pas and then write about them and, perhaps, spare you from some of the embarrassments and disappointments I've experienced.

While I'll elaborate more on all the gory details later on in this book, suffice it to say here that a few years ago I suffered a breakdown of sorts and went to a counselor for help. The treatment and cure surprised me, and I think it will surprise you too. Pure and simple, the medicine I needed was friends. That's right: friendship.

Who knew? Certainly not me. I had barely been seeing a therapist for a month when she remarked, "Lisa, you have the most elaborate defense mechanisms I've ever encountered. Your mind has created backup protections for just about any direction I attempt to reach your heart."

Thankfully, she wasn't daunted. She had a solution and a goal. "Your head has figured out a way to tell your heart that it isn't really feeling what it is feeling," she explained. "There will come a day when your heart will rebel and come screaming to the surface and tell your head to stop telling it what to think and how to feel." She discerned that there were some significant repressed memories and that my subconscious fortress would never give up its secrets until it had some outside support systems in place.

She suggested that we shelve for a season some of the issues that were presenting themselves and concentrate on creating a superstructure of supportive friends. She was all for digging at the roots, but her theory was that once I felt safe enough, many of the answers would offer themselves as I was ready.

So we spent the next few months talking about friendships, specifically, grown-up, female friendships. Yes, we certainly delved into the world of friendships with family members, but that is another story, not included in this book. So, if you notice a few missing lead characters like my husband, mother, father, brothers, and children, you're not imagining the gap. These relationships are left out on purpose. Friendships within family are a beautiful gift, but they involve nuances that would distract from my recent journey, which has been more specifically of the girlfriend kind.

Mostly, my counselor and I explored why it was difficult for me to allow friends to get close to me. We talked about how to identify safe people and how to implement boundaries. Through authentic conversation with my professional friend, I was learning how to be more honest and vulnerable and, thus, make a two-way connection possible.

We started by taking a good long look at my oldest friendships. They definitely reflected my head and heart split. But I learned never to underestimate the power of tears, need, brokenness, desire, grace, and love. I gingerly practiced vulnerability with my old friends and then tiptoed into opening myself up to the possibility of new friends.

Growing in Friendship

Within the context of relationships, I began to experience deep healing and to grow healthier, and that is what this book is really about. It is not a "how-to" book on making friends and creating lasting relationships. That is a worthy book, but I'm not qualified to write that one. Instead, I will simply share my story and hope that you will find yourself drawn in to join me on this journey. Where are we headed? I don't know exactly; I'm not there yet.

I am still in the beginning stages of learning how to connect at an intimate level. On a good day, I would say that I'm in the middle of the messy, mysterious part of a journey into friendship. That's okay. I have a sneaking suspicion that the mess and the mystery are essential to friendship for grown-ups—that friendship this side of heaven may not get any cleaner or clearer.

At one time or another, and all at the same time, friendship feels scary, hopeful, overwhelming, life-giving, aching, enriching, stretching, and oxymoronically like a deeply satisfying hunger. Relationships can cause us to feel off balance and out of control, which makes it so much easier to give up our clutching for self-sufficiency and to grasp onto the Lord in utter dependence.

So this isn't a book full of answers as much as it is replete with my questions. And yet . . .

There's one answer I don't question: God is much more able to lead you on your personal journey of friendship than I am. You are uniquely you. He knows exactly who you are and what you need and who can best meet your needs. Your process won't look exactly like mine any more than we both have the same basic features but probably look very different. Three things I do know probably for sure: God will lead you very personally and gently, the path won't be anything like you expect, and the walking out of his plan will take longer than anticipated.

And I am here to say it is worth it. For me, the last few years of learning about grown-up friendship have been difficult and painful, but I have so much growth to show for them. My heart has been broken, but that was a severe mercy. Without the brokenness, I couldn't have known my need. Without realizing my need, I wouldn't have risked reaching out to others. Without entering into relationship with others, I would have missed authentic connection.

With the vulnerability that comes with honest connection, I learned the importance of identifying safe people. Finding safe people cushioned me with love and courage to face conflict for the things that matter rather than choosing peace at any price. Learning conflict resolution skills made way for intimacy, and intimate friendship created an atmosphere of grace.

Grace, of course, ushered in self-acceptance. Embracing myself helped me believe and receive God's love. Resting in his delight changed me forever.

For years, I tried to get to an understanding of God's grace and love all by myself. But God had a different plan. He created us for relationship—not only with himself but also with others. If God the Father, Son, and Holy Spirit need each other, then where in the world did I get the impression that he was impressed with my Lone Ranger exploits?

The truth is I need friends.

There, I said it. That was hard. I don't like needing anything because to need feels dangerous and *is* dangerous. But the reward is nothing less than the possibility of intimacy with God, yourself, and others. In my opinion, that is the closest thing to Heaven on Earth.

Two

The Facts of My Life

O nce upon a time . . . and so begins my story-book childhood. I am the firstborn child of two parents who loved me. At the age of four, I became a big sister to an adorable baby brother. Along the way, we always had at least one beloved family dog.

As with all storybook tales, there was a mix of good and bad, dark and light, happy and sad. But until fairly recently, I could only allow myself to see the positive, look on the bright side, the glass is half-full perspective. I admit I've been a die-hard Pollyanna.

Well, I can't say the irrepressible optimist in me has died, but she's certainly facing some health challenges. Looking at the darker chapters of my childhood story has been a reluctant journey for me. I've been afraid of the dark, and I didn't dare go there alone. Thankfully, God sent wonderful friends to hold my hand and gently guide me along the way.

For instance, not long ago I was having tea with my friend Marilyn Meberg (who also happens to be a therapist). We were talking about my very public struggle with weight when I was on *The Facts of Life*. I got to the part in the story where I share how, during seasons two and three, my character, Blair, started gaining a lot of weight. (I'm going to blame Blair for packing on the extra pounds, so I don't have to take any personal responsibility for it.) As you can imagine, the producers weren't very happy. After all, they had cast me to play a character who looked a certain way (beautiful and thin), and I was quickly outgrowing that role (and my Eastland Academy uniform).

It didn't matter to the powers that be that I was simply a normal, developing sixteen-year-old girl trying to navigate a very awkward and confusing time of life, alone. I was living in Hollywood with my grandmother, and my parents were back in Texas in the middle of a gut-wrenching divorce. Like many teens, I turned to food for comfort and some semblance of control. (I'll just say that going through puberty is hard enough, but going through puberty on television is a whole other level.)

One afternoon, the president of the studio called me into his office. When I walked in, I noticed a scale in the middle of the floor. He told me to step onto the scale, and then he said, "You either lose the weight or lose your job."

Well, if any of you have any history with emotional eating, then you know exactly what I did next. I knocked on Nancy McKeon's dressing room door and said, "Come with me, I'm getting a cheeseburger." The way she remembers that particular lunch, there wasn't a fry left anywhere in sight.

Of course, the more I ate, the heavier I got. The heavier I got, the guiltier I felt. The guiltier I felt, the more I ate. It was a vicious cycle, and no matter how much resolve I woke up with, I couldn't stop overeating.

The studio heads determined that they must not have made themselves perfectly clear, so they threatened a little louder. From that point on, every morning when I walked through the rehearsal hall doors, I had to step onto the scales waiting in the middle of the room so that the producers and writers and director could see if I had gained or lost any weight that day.

It was at this point in our conversation when Marilyn must have put on her shrink hat when I wasn't looking because she interrupted: "Sweet Baby, how did that make you feel?" (By the way, if you've known Marilyn longer than five minutes, then you become "Sweet Baby" to her, which is one of the things I love most about her and that never fails to touch me tenderly.)

"I don't remember feeling anything," I answered honestly.

Marilyn gently and skillfully probed: "Well, if you could put words to what you think you might have been feeling, what would they be?"

Suddenly my feelings seemed crystal clear to me. "I felt like I deserved it," I confessed.

"Sweet Baby," Marilyn said, "what in your childhood set you up to believe that you deserved that kind of humiliation?"

This was the first time I had given much thought at all to my upbringing. After all, I had a storybook childhood, remember?

The truth is, this kind of situation felt perfectly normal and legitimate, which was Marilyn's point exactly.

Your Memories Mean Something

I have another psychologist friend, George, who shared something with me that was very intriguing. "Pay attention to your earliest memories," he said. "The reason you remember them is because they probably were accompanied by strong emotion. At the point when your heart was wide open, something happened, and from a child's perspective, a message was imprinted on your soul that you probably still live by today."

I immediately recalled my first memory. It was a picture of a purple folder full of pages I had colored for a nursery rhyme reciting class my mother signed me up for the summer I turned four years old. At the end of the six weeks, we had a recital and each student was to memorize and perform one nursery rhyme. The teacher found out that I had memorized all of the nursery rhymes, so she decided to put me on the program last, as the grand finale. I added a little choreography complete with large hand gestures and a big smile.

At the end of my performance, the room full of parents applauded. The joy of the moment opened up my little heart, and then I saw my daddy's face in the back of the room. *He's paying attention to me,* I thought. *He's smiling. I think he likes me.*

As we walked out of the dance studio, my mom carried me all around on her hip, and I realized, *She's proud of me.*

In those moments, it all made sense in my preschooler mind, and this was the message I wrote on my heart: "So this is how you get the love and attention and connection you so desperately crave. Don't just do what's expected of you. Do more than what's expected of you. And don't just do it a little bit. Do it really big . . . and with a smile!"

So that is how I've lived my life, dancing as fast as I can, smiling as big as I can to be noticed and prove myself worthy of love and connection. As a child, this meant attempting to be the perfect little girl. Once I started school, it meant making straight A's and being the teacher's pet.

In second grade, I discovered acting and beginning

with my very first drama class, I won the starring role in every play I auditioned for. At the age of ten, I trusted Jesus to forgive me of my sins by his grace, and then I promptly set out to earn his love by attempting to be the best Christian he had ever seen.

Many of my childhood memories are of being hyper-aware of never making a mistake. Yes, the punishment would be intense, but I felt like I deserved that. It was the break in connection with my primary source of life and love that caused me to feel terror. I know "terror" is a strong word, but as a child that is what disconnection felt like to me.

I would do anything to restore the bond. This meant I would assess the situation, try to figure out what I had done wrong, learn from my mistake, accept my punishment, determine to never mess up again, and then try really, really hard to be good so we could be close again.

Up until this point, my perception of a safe connection of love was based on not doing anything wrong to break the bond.

Missing My Childhood

In 1976, Walt Disney Productions decided to revise the television series *The Mickey Mouse Club*. (This is not the Mouseketeers from the fifties with Annette Funicello, and it's not the Club from the nineties with Britney Spears and

Justin Timberlake.) Don't worry if you didn't even know there was a New Mickey Mouse Club in the seventies. We often refer to ourselves as the forgotten mice.

After a nationwide talent search, I won the role and moved to Hollywood—without my family. My mom has often said, "What was I thinking? Letting you move off to California at the age of twelve? If I had it to do over again, I never would have let you audition." I guess none of us thought it all the way through to what would happen if I actually got the part on the show.

My mother flew out to Los Angeles with me and got me set up in the motel the studio provided for the twelve new Mouseketeers. But she soon needed to return home to Texas to take care of my eight-year-old brother, Cody. The whole family moving to California wasn't an option because my dad had just started his own business and he couldn't pull up stakes and start over in another state.

I lived with a variety of caregivers. My mother came as often as she could. Eventually, my grandmother joined the rotation. But for the most part, my mom found a handful of college girls and young women to be my guardians. For all intents and purposes, I was the one constant in my life.

But I was living my dream of being an actress, and I was capable of taking care of myself. I remember spreading out a newspaper on the kitchen table and looking for an apartment to move into. I was responsible for paying the utilities, and I learned early on how to balance my checkbook. I always knew when my "Call Time" was and where I needed to report for work. Out of necessity, I was the primary adult in my life.

You can read any "Where Are They Now?" story on former child stars and realize that growing up too fast is not healthy. There is a high price to pay for fame at an early age. The cost is nothing less than a childhood. We may not all manifest the effects of child sacrifice in overtly obvious ways, but my guess is that underneath every child star is a messed-up little kid wanting to grow down.

It was also during this time that I learned the hard way that just because someone is older and bigger than I am doesn't mean they can be trusted. I determined that it was not safe to be needy or vulnerable. There were many nights when I was scared and lonely, but I had to be big and brave.

I recently read a quotation that helped me understand what happened on the inside of me when I was being so strong on the outside. "Grief is a letting-down and a letting-go. And we cannot let down and let go if we are not being held up."[1]

I had no consistent connection with anyone to hold me up, so I held it all together. I built strong walls so I would be safe and so the pain would not break through and tear me apart from the inside out.

I believe this is how I survived. I cut off the desire for someone to always be there for me. I buried alive my child-ish needs and wishes. I had me, and I had Jesus. He was

19

my best friend and that was enough. Oh, I had other friends, but I never let them get too close.

After 186 episodes of *The New Mickey Mouse Club* were filmed, the show was canceled. I stayed in California to continue my acting career. For the next couple of years, I was cast in a handful of television shows and a couple of movies that went straight to video. In 1979, I got the part of Blair on the sitcom *The Facts of Life*, and the show ran for nine years on NBC.

Nancy, Kim, Mindy, and I filmed more than two hundred episodes until the series ended in 1988. We literally grew up together. We were definitely friends, but we were also coworkers. Each of us had her own life with separate friends after hours. I think there is a certain irony in the fact that the television show I was on was all about female friendships, and yet in real life I had very little experience with close relationships.

We filmed the last episode of *The Facts of Life* in March of 1988. I got married in July of '88. I got pregnant in '89. Then I had a child in '90, '91 and '92. So, obviously, Mrs. Garrett had taught me the "facts of life" well.

Acceptable Addictions

I left showbiz behind to become a stay-at-home wife and mother to three children in diapers. At the same time that

I was gaining baby weight, I was losing all the money I had made while working on television. Due to an economic downturn and a series of bad investments, we even lost our house and ended up living in a rented house on a pastor's salary.

As you can imagine, this put quite a strain on our young family. I wrote about our courtship, marriage, and newlywed years in my autobiography, *The Facts of Life and Other Lessons My Father Taught Me*. I won't rehearse all the details. Suffice it to say, my dating relationship with my husband began with an awkward lack of connection, and the stress of finances, babies, and our own brokenness brought even more disconnection.

Neither one of us knew how to access the deepest parts of our souls in order to experience intimacy. That felt too dangerous. Each of us had spent a lifetime keeping pain at bay behind walls and masks and roles. The problem with shutting down your emotions for self-protection is that there isn't an on-and-off switch to flip back on when you want.

The alternative was numbing my need with acceptable addictions. Thankfully, the busyness that comes with raising small children was the perfect antidote for feeling. I listened to the childhood message I had written on my heart and jumped into being the best wife and mother who ever lived. Actually, even that wasn't enough: I had to be a pastor's wife and homeschooling mother. Of course, I had to do everything more and bigger and with a smile.

Intuitively, I knew I needed support. My marriage was imploding, my finances had blown up, and my children were shrapnel. I needed help. I reached out to make friends as best I could. I called a couple of friends from my church. I invited them to come over on Friday. We could put our kids down for a nap, I would fix lunch, and we could play a game. We knew we had to make this a weekly tradition when we realized that after two hours of food and friendship, we liked being moms again, even after our kids woke up.

We eventually grew to become a handful of moms meeting weekly to eat and play games. We called ourselves The Good Medicine Club because laughter is such good medicine. And it was. In a self-preserving way, it was also easier for me to connect on a light-hearted level by keeping the focus on the games than to risk deep conversation that might sneak a peek behind the curtain of shame.

I was adept at appearing transparent without being vulnerable. There is a difference. Interestingly, once I started writing books and my blog, I often heard from my closest friends that they knew more about me from reading about me than they did from knowing me personally. It has always been easier for me to share my heart from a stage than it is to open up in a one-on-one conversation.

Writing was a perfect way to keep enough space to feel safe. My desire was to connect intimately, but I had no idea how to go about doing that in real life. It was like I could only get so close and then I would get scared and retreat behind "unflappable Lisa." Psychologist Henry Cloud nailed it in his book *Changes That Heal* when he wrote, "You can move toward others, get socially involved, and have relationships, but still be isolated."[2]

The best way to describe it is to say there was this wall of Plexiglass between me and the people I longed to be close to. I could put my hands up to the window of their souls to touch them, but I couldn't feel them.

Little did I know that if I could have fast-forwarded a few years, I would have seen that God was planning to shatter that wall.

Three

It's Okay to Be Needy

*I*t started innocently enough, just a couple of years ago, with a sweet little get-together on a classic front porch in Franklin, Tennessee. I had recently written a Bible study for LifeWay Publishers. The Women's Ministries Department had the delightful idea of hosting a lunch for all of their authors. I was beyond myself excited because my favorite author in the whole wide world, Beth Moore, was going to be attending. I didn't end up sitting at her table, but I did get to talk to her. I was starstruck.

As we wrapped up lunch, we were handed a little bag and told to reach in and draw out a bracelet with an attached prayer request card. It was explained to us that we were to pray for the person whose bracelet we selected and at the end of the summer we should mail the bracelet to them, having brought their desires before the Lord over the preceding three months.

The bracelet with my name on it was randomly chosen by Priscilla Shirer. When I look back at the beginning of this friendship and recognize God's sovereign hand, I am speechless. It just so happened that I had only recently moved from California to within thirty minutes of where she lived in Dallas, Texas.

The summer came and went, and I hadn't received my bracelet in the mail. As fall approached, I received an e-mail from Priscilla suggesting that since we lived so close, we should meet for dinner and she would hand me my bracelet personally. I loved that idea!

Steve and I met Priscilla and her husband, Jerry, and I don't think the guys got more than a word or two in all evening. Early on in the conversation, Priscilla discovered that Steve worked at Jack Hayford's church, and she had recently discovered his teaching and was really growing in the Lord and stretching her borders a bit.

By dessert, we recognized that we shared two important things. We were both extremely hungry to know the Lord in an experiential way, and we could share the journey of that experience because our foundation of faith was similar. She told me about a home Bible study she had been attending and invited me to go with her. I was thrilled. From all she told me, it was everything I had been longing for in a community of believers.

In actuality, it was everything and more. I fell in love with my Thursday mornings with the Lord. Oh my goodness, it was delicious. King David knew what he was talking about when he wrote in Psalm 34:8, "Taste and see that the LORD is good." The first forty-five minutes were spent listening to beautiful praise music while soaking in the Lord's presence by worshiping however we felt comfortable. That could mean everything from clapping and singing to sitting quietly in a comfy chair.

Next we enjoyed powerful and practical Bible teaching from the leaders, Mary Elaine and George. The last thirty minutes were set aside for prayer. And by prayer, I mean conversation with God, as in speaking and listening. I learned to recognize God's voice and presence in a profoundly personal way.

One day, after sensing his love in such a visceral way that I felt like every cell of my body was filled with his Spirit, I cried out to him in a whisper, "Oh, Lord, I want to bring this to the women I write for and speak to. I want them to experience such an encounter with your love that it goes beyond knowledge and settles into their very being."

I heard him gently respond: *I would love that too. The problem is, that wall you have built around your heart to protect yourself from getting hurt is the same wall that will prohibit my love from flowing out of you and onto others.*

Without hesitation I proclaimed, "Then tear that wall down!"

I had no idea what I was proclaiming. In answer to my prayer, God orchestrated the perfect storm. Within a few months, life was coming at me from all sides: mentally, emotionally, physically, and spiritually. Looking back, I see how God had to hit me from every angle in order to crack the wall I had designed with elaborate defense mechanisms.

The Perfect Storm

I have always been incredibly strong. I thought that was a good thing. In many ways, it is. But, in this case, it meant that in order to break through my ability to live in denial, numb my feelings, veneer my fear with platitudes, and stay one step ahead of pain intellectually, God had a plan to cover all bases.

Mentally, my mind already had enough to think about. I was past due on two writing deadlines, one for a how-to book on Bible study and the other an actual Bible study that incorporated journaling and scrapbooking. One project was doable, the two together were *ginormous*. I felt like I was at the base of Mount Everest and I was already out of breath.

Emotionally, I was completely drained. I was home-schooling three high schoolers (which meant I was also parenting three teenagers). Spiritually? Well, I'll have to resort to a distinctly Southern phrase: I was just "plumb give-out" from traveling and speaking at churches every weekend.

The final demolition ball slam was physical. Due to a freak mix-up with some of my husband's medicine, my hormones got all out of whack, which meant I was off balance and couldn't figure out if I was coming or going.

Needless to say, the wall was weak in places and was vulnerable if attacked in just the right spot. Of course, God knew exactly where that spot was and how to penetrate it, even if ever so slightly. Who would have ever guessed that his battering ram would be a tender moment of vulnerability from a friend?

One weekend, in the middle of the storm, I was speaking at a women's event with my friend Angela Thomas. On Saturday night after the event was over, my husband and I invited a small group of people to join us for dinner, including Angela and her road manager, Lisa.

As the initial chitchat died down, I suggested, "Why don't we go around the table and each tell what God is teaching us during this season of life?"

When it came time for Angela to share, her eyes welled up with tears. "I am learning that it is okay to be needy," she said softly, "that God isn't surprised at me for wanting someone to love me and care for me. That these wants and needs are part of his design."

Oh my goodness! I can't imagine that every person in that restaurant didn't hear the earthquake that shook the foundation of my heart and caused the tiniest crack in my carefully constructed fortress of strength and self-protection. What? It was okay to be needy? The truth that Angela had just shared had never once crossed my mind in my whole life.

Henry Cloud writes, "Realization of need is the beginning of growth. Humility and vulnerability are absolutely necessary for bonding to take place at a deep level."[1]

I believe I began to grow in that moment of realization. I dared to humbly acknowledge my longing for connection, but I had no idea how to risk vulnerability. I wasn't even aware that I had needs. Please, don't hear that as arrogance. All my life, I had carefully avoided wanting and needing in order to spare myself the inevitable disappointment when those desires wouldn't be met. It just hurt less not to need. I could even fool myself into thinking I was super spiritual if I buried the needs so deep that I didn't even realize they were there.

Unfortunately, this was one of the very reasons I wasn't able to bond at a deep level with friends, even dear friends I had loved for years.

About six weeks after Angela's confession and, subsequently, the devastating run-in with the realization of my need, I was invited to join four of my oldest friends for a weekend in the mountains of Georgia. We hadn't seen each other since I'd moved to Texas, and we had lots to catch up on. One of the girls, Shelly, is a gourmet cook, so we stopped for groceries on the way to the cabin and then never set foot out the door or out of our pajamas again until it was time to go home. The only thing on the agenda was to eat and talk for two whole days.

Now, this is my idea of heaven! I was so excited to be invited. I loved and respected each of these women and was giddy at the thought of just being with them. The first day, we took turns sharing what was going on in our lives, where we were in our journeys, the ups and downs, challenges and triumphs. Each person ended up talking for about four hours, so by the end of the first day, we had only heard from two women. It was a rich, rich time of sharing.

Nobody knew, but I was painfully aware of feeling like an observer the whole time. It felt like I was on the outside looking in. Oh, this had nothing to do with the welcoming of me from my friends. They were incredibly embracing. I realized this was completely my problem.

As I watched the other women interact, I noticed how they were able to really be there for each other, body, soul, and spirit. They laughed with abandon, touched generously, and when one expressed sadness, they all shed tears. Except me. I realized that it had been years since I had shed a tear. I sat there longing to connect with these friends on an emotional level but not having a clue how to even begin.

That night, when I retired to my bedroom, I asked God with a deep sense of shame and embarrassment, "What's the matter with me? Why can't I feel? Why can't I cry?" He answered me immediately. I knew it was him because his voice was so gentle (when I talk to myself, I tend to sound much more critical and correcting).

He tenderly whispered to my heart, *Little one, I'm not mad at you for building that wall around your heart. It was my protection for you as a little girl. But it is safe to come out now.*

His words took away my breath, and I thought: *You mean there is hope that I could be different? Are you saying that this isn't just the way I am? I might be able to feel deeply? I might be able to connect at a heart level with a friend?*

A New Friend

It was a perfect setup for the entrance of a new friendship. Within weeks of returning home from that little weekend getaway, I was asked to help with a fund-raising event for our homeschooling group. The coordinator was a long, tall glass of Texas sweet tea named Heather. It was immediately obvious why she was dubbed the leader of this mammoth undertaking. She had all the qualities necessary to be head of a volunteer committee: talent and the inability to say no.

The more we worked together, the more I both admired her and felt sorry for her. As the weeks marched on toward the night of the big gala, she gained my respect at every turn. She was not only extremely bright, organized and creative, she was also funny, caring, and sincerely sweet. I thought to myself, I'd really like to get to know her.

Once the event was behind us, I invited her to meet me at Starbucks one Wednesday night while my kids were at church. As I listened to her story, my heart broke for her. She was under so much stress and yet never once complained. Her husband was a painter by trade, but a couple of years ago he fell off of some scaffolding and had to have back surgery. He never fully recovered; they had been living on disability ever since, and he had been unable to find a job. She had two young children and was homeschooling the kindergartener in the evenings while working full time at a brand new job where she felt completely in over her head. She was struggling to handle more than her fair share of life's hard knocks, yet she always had a ready word of affirmation to offer a friend in need.

While Heather was carrying the weight of the world on her shoulders, I was not yet in touch with my feelings. I was in my *c'est la vie* modus operandi. (You didn't know I was multilingual, did ya?) I found out later after our Starbucks visit that Heather had said to God, "I would really like to have a friend like Lisa. She's strong and funny and couldn't care less what other people think about her. I would love to be that confident and secure."

If Heather had only known that the countdown clock

was already ticking and that painted wall of confident strength, also known as a façade, was already on its way down. But, at this point, there was still only a tiny crack in the plaster.

Apparently, that was enough.

Somehow, Heather got inside behind the wall and next to my heart. I started to really care about her and her family and her life. I wanted to help her and be there for her. I realized that I really wanted to be her friend.

This terrified me. I wasn't used to these feelings. I was Miss Independent. I didn't like the thought of wanting someone to like me. What if she discovered that I wasn't really that strong and confident? Then she would have the power and the right to reject me. I hated feeling so vulnerable.

She was so sweet and unthreatening. This was ridiculous. Why was I making such a big deal about having a new friend? But this was different, and I knew it. The foreign feelings were more frightening than the situation warranted. In a brave moment, I confessed my fears to her, "I'm scared to death to enter into this friendship." She reassured me, "Well, I'm not scared. Trust me. Jump on into the deep end; the water's fine." I laughed off my insecurity with a little joke, "Okay, I'll jump in, but I'm keeping on my Floaties!"

The perfect storm had crashed through the walls, and I found myself struggling to keep my head above the pool of pain. One minute I felt like I was drowning in need, and the next minute I inhaled such a deep gasp of fresh air that it felt like I had never breathed before.

All of a sudden, years and years of tears came flooding out of my soul. Where did they all come from? And why were they coming out now, all at one time? Heather couldn't have been the reason I was crying. I barely knew her. Was it just a coincidence that, after she invited me to jump into the waters of friendship, I began to feel like I was sinking in a sea of emotions?

Many months later, I read something that I surely wished I had found earlier because I just thought I was getting weird:

> Whenever you begin to allow someone to matter to your isolated heart, uncomfortable needy and dependent feelings will surface. These are the beginnings of a softening heart. Though uncomfortable, these feelings are a key to attachment. Many times you think you need to "keep a stiff upper lip" but allowing your tender, needy sides to show to the ones you need will cement the attachment and allow it to grow.[2]

Instinctively, I guess I knew this, because I began to open up and risk being vulnerable and needy. One afternoon, in particular, I was dog-paddling in waves of emotion that threatened to pull me under. I was supposed to be at the library writing a book, but I couldn't brush the tears off my face fast enough to spare myself embarrassment with the library visitors, so I retreated to my minivan and crouched in the backseat to have a good cry.

I called out to God and begged him to speak to me, "What is happening to me? Why am I so afraid? Please, come rescue me. Where are you?" In my mind's eye, as plain as day, I saw the words *Jeremiah 31:3*. I couldn't wait to get my Bible out of the glove compartment of my car to read what I hoped was an answer to my cry.

I was not prepared for his answer. That particular scripture says, *I have loved you with an everlasting love; I have drawn you with loving-kindness*. In that one verse, God answered my deepest question. I knew in that moment that he was with me in the middle of this storm and all that was happening was motivated by his love for me.

I was so happy that God had met me in my need that my first thought was that I wanted to call Heather and tell her about it. That felt odd to me. Why did I want to share this with her? Then the negative thoughts started rolling: *What if I call her and she's busy? What if she thinks I'm weird?* Ugh! I hated caring so much about what somebody thought of me.

The desire for connection, though, was stronger than the desire to be safe, so I picked up my cell phone and dialed Heather's number.

She couldn't have been more accepting and affirming. She said it sounded just like the kind of thing God would do for a daughter he adored.

After a very easy conversation, I confessed my initial trepidation at the thought of calling her.

She laughed, but not mockingly, "Why would you ever worry about calling me? I love to talk to you."

In a moment of stark honesty, I said, "I don't want to need you. I know you have so many friends and you don't need one more, and I feel so needy."

"Oh, Lisa." Heather met my honesty with her own: "I do have lots of friends, but none that I would dare need. We could have stumbled onto the kind of friendship that comes around once in a lifetime. Don't be afraid to need me. I want to be a safe place for you to fall."

From that point on, I wanted to share everything with her. I wanted to tell her my story, to know and be known. She was busy and I was too, but suddenly this was like water in a desert. I just wanted to drink in as much of this friendship as time would allow. This connection was like a source of life to my parched soul.

In hindsight, I see how I reverted to childhood patterns. My old self wasn't going to pack up and leave so easily. I thought that the way to stay connected with someone you needed was to make the other person happy and that the best way to do that was to give a lot and need little in return. So, once again, I made myself indispensable.

As was my custom, I determined that I would be the best friend she ever had. I prayed for her often, even fasting when she was facing a giant obstacle at work. I sat with her in the waiting room through her husband's multiple surgeries. I grew to know and love her children.

Most of all, I tried my hardest to love her the way the Bible talks about when John 15:13 (ESV) says, "Greater love has no one than this, that someone lay down his life for his friends."

I also fell into my old routine of performing to earn love. I suffered this internal struggle of wanting to be seen and accepted just the way I am, but deep down I was afraid that wasn't good enough. I worried that she would discover the truth and reject me, so I did my best to impress her and prove that I was worthy of her friendship.

I barely recognized myself. *Who was this person I was becoming?* One minute, I was a blubbering idiot, desperate for her attention, and the next minute I was showing off and hanging up my Grammy nomination on the wall of my office so she would see it when she came over to visit. I would go from being a downright braggadocio to being so shy I could barely say a word for fear I would say the wrong one and she wouldn't like me anymore. Yikes! Life was so much easier when I couldn't feel.

I didn't want easier anymore. I had experienced feeling, and there was no going back, only deeper, and the only way out was through.

How People Grow

As providence would have it, I was given the book *How People Grow* by Henry Cloud and John Townsend. It was like reading a book about a foreign land. Fascinating and compelling, but distant and unreachable. They talked about things I had never heard of and some places I'd read about all my life but never thought I'd want to live there.

The gist of the book is the importance of relationships and how God is relational and has created us in his image. The premise is that growth happens within the context of community. I knew that God was leading me to a new level of growth and it could only happen within intimate relationship. With each word I read, it felt like a flashlight was shining on the next step I was to take on my journey:

> Stay connected, don't isolate. We tend to withdraw from relationship when we are hurt. Some people are afraid of their dependencies on others. Others feel guilty about burdening friends with their problems. Still others try to be self-sufficient. None of these responses helps a person heal and grow.[3]

Wow! God was climbing out of the box I had him so neatly contained in. I had lived my life thinking that God was all I needed and that I shouldn't need other people because if I looked to people to meet my needs, that would be idolatry. Now here God was, very clearly saying to me that if I wanted to grow deeper in my relationship with him, then it required entering into close relationships, acknowledging my need, and allowing myself to depend on others.

I inhaled these ideas and saturated the pages of the book with my yellow highlighter. One passage, in particular, I highlighted, underlined, starred, and circled!

> The clear teaching of the New Testament is that the body of Christ is to be people deeply connected to each other, supporting each other, and filling each other's hearts.[4]

This is it! I thought. *This is what I want! This is what I was made for!* I determined to dedicate the next season of my life to understanding and experiencing intimacy with God, myself, and others.

I knew immediately that this process would take more time than I currently had available. I mean, I had a daily habit of praying and reading my Bible in the mornings, but to experience intimacy with Jesus, I longed for unhurried moments to simply be with him and to think and listen.

There was no room on my calendar for time to share a leisurely lunch with a friend, even if I had no more than one close friend. I had studiously, yet subconsciously, avoided time to get to know myself. Yuck. I was so busy constructing an acceptable image of who I thought I should be that I certainly didn't want to slow down long enough to catch a glimpse of the less-than-perfect me.

Here was my dilemma. I had, only a few weeks prior, turned in the Bible study and manuscript for my last two projects. I had another installment in The Motherhood Club series of books (*The Busy Mom's Guide to . . .*) due within the next six months, and I still had one major book left on my three-book contract with another publisher.

It seemed there wasn't one minute available on my calendar to develop intimacy for at least another year. I didn't want to wait that long. I felt the distinct impression that I was to go on a one-year sabbatical from writing. I thought to myself, if I can hunker down and write the book, maybe I can postpone writing the other book and then I can take off a year to understand what it means to enter into a true sabbath rest (something I obviously knew nothing about).

As it turned out, God was way ahead of me. One publishing company was bought out by another publisher, so I was able to be amicably released from the obligation to write the last book (Motherhood Club series) in that contract. Within weeks, my other publisher asked me if I could change the focus of the book I was planning to write. I didn't feel equipped to write the book they requested, so I offered to step down so someone else could write it. It was a win-win situation for everyone.

Don't you just love it when God is up to something?

I had also been writing a monthly column for *Today's Christian Woman*, a print magazine now online only. Wouldn't you know it, the editorial team decided to overhaul the content of the magazine during this time and no longer needed my input. The only thing left to resolve was my Web site journal.

Before there was even the word *blog*, I was blogging. I called it Coffee Talk and I simply shared my life with my Internet friends. This was the hardest thing to give up because I felt like they were my little flock, and I had a deep sense of commitment to be a faithful steward of the influence God had given me in their lives. But I knew that I needed to eliminate even good things to make room for the God thing.

Within days, I felt like I was going through withdrawal. And, in a very real way, I was indeed. I discovered very quickly that working had become my drug of choice. I had written thirteen books in the last six years. Once I stopped working so furiously, the pain came screaming to the surface, and the issues beneath it were close behind. I needed help, and I needed it right away. I had just taken another step toward my inevitable breakdown.

Four

A Merciful Breakdown

With workaholism no longer an option, I divided my time between contacting friends to have lunch, reading every book I could get my hands on, exercising, and crying—mostly crying.

So many memories and emotions were rushing to the surface. My feelings were all tangled up. I couldn't tell why I was even crying most of the time. The one thing that seemed to bring me the most relief was talking to Heather. I felt like a pressure cooker, and whenever I could express some of the steam from the water boiling under the lid, I felt better. There was just so much bubbling up, and I wanted to process aloud with her. I wanted to tell her everything.

Even my secrets. I thought: *So this must be what it feels like to have a best friend.*

I was becoming aware of things that I had chosen to ignore. Denial was loosening its hold, and reality was frightening. I didn't want to face it alone. Heather assured me that she wanted to be my "friend for the journey."

I tried to be careful not to burden her with my problems because she was dealing with so many heavy issues in her own life. I wanted to be strong for her so she could lean on me. I knew she was almost to the end of a huge deadline at work. If I could just hold on until she had that pressure behind her then, perhaps, I could lean on her for a while. We both said we believed that God had sent us to each other because he didn't want us to have to walk our difficult paths alone.

As much as she wanted to be there for me, her new job, children, and housebound husband, understandably, required most of her time and more energy than she had on hand. Without work to fill my emptiness and with Heather unavailable, I had to find an additional addiction to distract me. Of course, it had to be an acceptable one. After all, I still was speaking to Christian women's groups on the weekends. So I found the perfect solution: exercise.

It looked so innocent. As a matter of fact, I was affirmed and applauded for my self-discipline. I exercised like a maniac. Some mornings, I was at our neighborhood fitness center when the doors opened at five o'clock to run on the treadmill for an hour. I also hired a personal trainer to work out with weights twice a week. I lost twenty-five pounds in six months. One morning, I stepped out of the bathtub and caught a glimpse of myself in the mirror. I thought: *I've always struggled with my weight. I've exercised before and still couldn't drop a pound. What's different about this time?*

As clear as a bell, I heard the Lord impress upon my heart: *You're not going to need that protection anymore.*

Instantly, I knew what he was referring to, but I had never told anyone about it, until a few weeks later when I met Heather for dinner and shared my secret. We were talking in the car before I left the restaurant. I told her about what I felt the Lord had said to me. Then I confessed, "There is sexual abuse in my past, and I know I'm going to have to deal with it someday."

Heather was compassionate, but she apparently didn't know how to respond. So she didn't say much, and I drove away.

The next morning, I woke up crying and stayed in bed crying all day. I had never spoken those words out loud, and from what I've learned since that time, something deep happens when your brain hears you say something out loud that doesn't happen when you simply think it. It was as if the power of those words acted like a wrecking ball and knocked another huge hole into my wall.

I kept waiting for Heather to call and check on me, but

she was busy at work. I knew that and I understood, but in my regressed state, it felt like rejection to me. This seemed to be happening much more often. It felt like the more I needed her, the more she withdrew from me. At the same time, she didn't seem to need me as much anymore.

Her job had leveled out a bit, she put her kids back into public school, and best of all, her widowed mother decided to move to Dallas to help her with the load. This was a huge answer to prayer, and I was thrilled for Heather. I was also aware that her mother was her best friend—and there was increasingly less room for me in her friend basket.

Grieving Has Many Faces

It was during this season of my journey that a dear friend, and past editor, of mine came through Dallas. As I sat across the table from Philis at The Cheesecake Factory, I was excruciatingly embarrassed. I could barely string two sentences together without choking on my tears. With an understanding born of experience, she reached across the table, held my hand, and softly said, "You're grieving, Lisa."

"Grieving? Grieving what? Nobody died."

Philis clarified: "My guess is you are grieving losses from long, long ago. The hurt may feel present and may even be tied to situations you are experiencing now, but the tears are old."

A week later, I received probably the sweetest gift I've ever been sent in the mail. Philis sent me a box of comfort that included two mugs with an assortment of tea bags, a lovely journal, a comfy throw blanket, two boxes of moisturized Kleenex, and some chocolate. She was right. I was grieving, and I needed the comfort of a friend.

Heather, though, wasn't there. In fact, she was very definitely pulling away. I could rarely catch her on the phone. We had most of our conversations via text messaging. I suggested that we not wait until we had a long space of time to talk. That would probably never "just happen" in the midst of our busy lives. Maybe we could simply touch base everyday with a little three-minute conversation. That way, we wouldn't get so far behind and then have so much to talk about and never enough time to catch up.

We never did seem to find time to connect though. It hurt so badly. Heather said she wanted to walk this journey with me, but she wouldn't even return my phone calls. Then when we finally would connect, she acted like nothing was wrong and we were still BFFs—Best Friends Forever.

True, I know I overwhelmed Heather with my neediness. Trust me, I hated myself for needing her friendship. I truly wished I had more friends close by so that I could have spread the love load.

I got really scared. I felt ashamed and embarrassed, like I was making a fool of myself. I kept thinking I loved too big and too much. I even worried that I was committing idolatry by turning to Heather instead of God. In reality, I was still utterly devoted to God, but my old imaginary tapes were playing in my ear, telling me that anyone I turned to other than God would become a lower-case god.

Hindsight is 20-20. I wish I had simply been thankful for all the wonderful qualities Heather shared with me. There was so much to be grateful for in our friendship. If only I had been content with what she was able to offer. But at that point in my life, I needed more than she had to give. And the deficit tapped into deep memories of longing and inconsistent connection.

So, I came up with a way to silence my need. I wrote Heather an e-mail explaining that I suspected I had become emotionally dependent on her. I knew God was doing a deep work of healing in my soul, and I had a sneaking suspicion that I was attempting to self-medicate the pain by turning to our friendship the way an alcoholic would turn to drink or a drug addict to drugs. If that were the case, which I believed it probably was, the only way to deal with a dependency was by going cold turkey.

I told her that I didn't want to be addicted to anything, even something as seemingly innocent as a friendship. I expressed my deep sorrow that I had failed at being "the best friend she ever had." I had really thought I could be such a friend, but I was wrong. I asked her to give me time and space to allow God to heal my wounds and fill my longings. It was my hope that in the future I would be able to be the kind of selfless friend she deserved.

The break I tried lasted for less than two weeks.

I didn't want to lose this friendship. I came up with a plan. I would resume the friendship, but I determined as an act of my will not to need her as much anymore. Which meant I still felt rejected when it was obvious that she was moving on in her life without me, but I wasn't going to let her know that. I was just fine, thank you very much, and living a rich, full life.

I retreated behind my wall, put on my dancing shoes and party mask, and gave a performance worthy of best actress in a supporting role nomination.

Well, unless you count the nonstop crying.

Getting Help

As much as I wanted to be strong and brave and independent, I needed help and I needed it right away. I needed a friend to share my burdens even if I had to pay someone to listen to me. I made some phone calls and found a place where I could go for a week of outpatient intensive therapy.

For six straight days, I had back-to-back counseling sessions from 7:00 a.m. until 9:00 p.m. No two sessions were the same. Some of them were with individual doctors, but many of them were in a group setting.

It surprised me how much I loved group sessions! I had never experienced anything before quite like them. *This*, I thought, *is what I wish church felt like.* There were three to ten people in any given group setting, and we were each very different yet all broken, so immediately we were on equal footing. I met a major league baseball pitcher, a scientist, a pastor, a single mother, a gay lawyer, a ritual abuse survivor, and an elementary school teacher. Within days, and a handful of group sessions, I loved each one of these people and felt closer to them than to many friends I'd known for decades.

In my very first group meeting, I learned that I was afraid of feeling. I was scared that my emotions were too big and that they would get so out of control that I might do something wrong. It felt unsafe to feel strong emotions. I realized that I would rather research extensively, determine the correct path to take, and then by the strength of my will, do the right thing. Cutting out my heart seemed to guarantee that I wouldn't make as many mistakes.

That theme surfaced throughout the week. I was terrified of making a mistake. My association with messing up was punishment, but even worse than that, disconnection from love. It was too painful. Participating in a group setting offered me a safe environment to feel deep emotions for other people when I couldn't yet risk experiencing painful memories or feelings for myself.

One of my favorite group sessions was Awareness Group. Through a series of exercises, our counselor led us through a handful of experiences designed to heighten our awareness of everyday moments. My favorite assignment was to eat a piece of candy using the full spectrum of senses, as if it were the very first time I had ever tasted chocolate.

Then we were directed to listen to a song that our counselor played for us and to become aware of and then enter into the emotions that the song evoked and brought to the surface. Finally, we were to follow our responses.

At first, the song elicited pleasant feelings. I don't know what the song title is or who sings it, and I haven't been able to find it since, but I remember how the lyrics affected me. The song went something like this: "I know I can't rescue you, but I will stay beside you and be in the pain with you." So as I listened to it, I began to feel sadness and discouragement, because that has been what I desperately wanted in my life—someone to be with me and share my pain. Suddenly I felt hopeful when I realized that I can be that friend to myself. I can be here for me, comfort me, walk beside me, and God can and will too.

Then the intensity of the song changed to a forceful tempo, and it disturbed me. It made me mad for disturbing this peaceful place. I wanted to shut it down and get away from it. Instead, I made the choice to fully experience and befriend the negative emotions of anger and anxiety. I felt them fully. Even in my body. Then I released them. In not fighting them, I was able to let them go. The end of the song was a very catchy chorus, and I felt the urge to dance.

For a moment, I understood the healing that could happen if I ever felt fully free to dance as if no one were watching.

We took turns sharing our feelings and observations. It is amazing to me how much you can get to know someone in such a short time when you go beyond small talk. Whether we talked about eating chocolate or entering into a song or blowing bubbles, I felt like I was truly knowing and being known, and there was tremendous opportunity for intimacy and connection with strangers who were quickly becoming friends.

I may have learned the most in my codependency group. For starters, I really had no idea what the term meant. I thought it had something to do with being married to a drug addict. Come to find out, it was a ton more complicated than that, and I was in exactly the perfect group for me even though my husband barely takes the occasional Tylenol.

I don't think I ever fully understood all of the nuances of the term, but the notes I took described codependency this way.

1. It is an emotional disease manifested by dysfunctional behaviors and an ability to tolerate a lot of pain. (Check)

    I was learning that much of what I had thought was laying down my life for others was often translated as "walk all over me and I'll keep smiling and trying harder to please."

2. It is characterized by emotional immaturity. (Check.)

In shutting down my deep emotions at an early age, I got stuck there. One of the reasons I was afraid of my intense feelings is because I still felt like a small child with emotions that threatened to overpower me. I needed to remember that I was a grown woman with little girl emotions. It was important for me to grow through my feelings, not stuff them somewhere out of sight. Unfortunately, responding like a five-year-old while living in a forty-five-year-old body is not always welcomed, unless you are in a group setting. Just one more reason I was falling in love with "group."

3. It is an emotional disease of control. (Check.)

I lived the majority of my life in my head and in my will. To be in touch with my heart and my body felt dangerous and held the possibility of being out of control. That wasn't an option. Bad things happened when I opened my heart or listened to my body. To be a good Christian and to maintain a safe environment, I must always be in control. That was the message by which I ran my life.

4. It is an emotional disease of extremes. (Check.)

I had always prided myself on being an all-or-nothing kind of girl. Anything I got involved in, I jumped into with both feet. Looking back, I can see that I often got lost in a project or hobby in much the same way that an addict gets lost to a drug. By being so extreme, I could distract myself from feelings that might otherwise find space to creep up. I could also attempt mastery which could offer me the phantom reward of control. All-or-nothing also eliminated the messy mysterious middle. That place felt way too insecure.

5. It is an emotional disease of shame. (Nah, not me.)

I had certainly done things I regretted, and, yes, I felt like a fool lately with all my tears and dependency issues. But shame? Nah. Turns out, shame was truly at the root, but I didn't dare acknowledge it because then I might have actually had to look at the cause of it.

I guess it is unrealistic to think you can go to a place like this and not uncover some stuff you've attempted to cover up. At times, I felt like I was visiting the eye doctor, seeing things like I'd never seen them before. It was strange. There were so many things in my life that I had only seen from my perspective, usually the perspective of a child, and that is the view I had of them for the rest of my life. Now my counselors and friends from my group sessions were opening my eyes to newer, truer ways of looking at my life.

The Purpose of a Broken Heart

I came home from that week of round-the-clock counseling physically and emotionally drained. I felt like a wet noodle.

I weighed less than I had since before I got married, and I walked around like a weak kitten. But there is also a strength that comes from facing pain and surviving. I wanted to live the rest of my life with courage to press through truth rather than insulate myself from harsh realities.

The first brave step I needed to take was to have an honest conversation with Heather.

Melodramatic as this might sound, I was scared to death—not scared of Heather, for she is a gentle soul. I was afraid that if I were honest with her about my feelings of disappointment and perceptions of rejection, then she would be mad at me, not like me anymore, and no longer want to be my friend.

My nature is not that of a fighter, and I hate conflict of any kind. The thought of purposely confronting Heather, a friend I cared about, felt like suicide, even if it were simply sharing my hurt feelings. In reality, choosing peace at any cost over being real meant I had been killing my true self for years.

I had been home from the counseling center for about a week when I met Heather at Starbucks to debrief my week of therapy. While I had been away, we hadn't communicated. Every night when I returned to my hotel, I longed for a girlfriend to talk to about everything I was experiencing. I received a text message from her midweek to tell me she was praying for me, but that was the extent of her touch.

What was ironic was the fact that before Heather had her change of heart about our friendship, she said to me, "Maybe you could find a place to go away for a week to find help to process all these tangled emotions and repressed memories. I could go with you and be there for emotional support."

During my counseling week, I wondered what I had done wrong to cause her to go from that kind of friendship commitment to a Heisman Trophy-type pushback.

After counseling, I had better vision to see things the way they really were, not just the way I wished them to be. With my new eyesight, it was clear that Heather had been wonderful with words, and I believe they came from her heart, but she wasn't able to live out what she'd said.

It came time in our conversation to address this particular issue. Thankfully, she made it easy to begin by asking, "Did any of your counselors have anything to say about our friendship?" This was an understandable question. We both sensed, even though neither one of us had talked about it, that our relationship was deteriorating and that realization was causing me anguish.

I held my breath, silently prayed a quick *Help me, Jesus* and tiptoed into the truth. "Well, as a matter of fact," I began, "the head of the counseling center felt it was very important for me to express to you some of my perceptions and feelings about our friendship." I took another deep breath to keep going. "Heather, I put weight on your words.

When you told me that you wanted to be a friend for the journey, I assumed that meant you wanted to walk close beside me, not just check in every once in a while. I believed you when you said that you wanted to be a safe place for me to fall. And then when I let myself fall, because I felt safe to let go, you weren't there. I understand you are juggling so many important balls in your life, and inevitably, some of them are going to fall to the ground before you can catch them. I just need to tell you that this hurts."

I looked at her, and it was as if there had been a kind of shift in our world, like when C.S. Lewis's Lucy stepped through the wardrobe into the invisible realm of Narnia or when Lewis Carroll's Alice slid down the rabbit hole into Wonderland. I don't know how else to describe the sensation of that moment, but I knew things would no longer be the same.

With tears in her eyes, Heather responded, "Well, I guess I wrote an emotional check I was not able to cash."

From that moment, everything changed.

Heather had made the decision to completely cut me out of her life. I was ready and willing to forgive and move on, but her mind was made up. The next morning, she called and said out loud what I had already heard in the silence: "Lisa, I think it would be better if you found another best friend."

I tried to explain to her that the only reason I brought up my disappointments was so that we could get it out in the light and talk about it. I thought that our friendship could be strengthened, not severed, by honesty.

Heather made it clear that there was no chance for reconciliation when she confessed: "Lisa, I feel like I am letting down everyone in my life. I don't have enough to go around. I need to focus on my future and my family. You need too much from me. You're too heavy. You cry all the time. I'm at a point in my life when things are looking brighter, and I need happy, happy, joy, joy around me."

That which I feared the most had come upon me. Heather wanted to be my friend when I was strong, confident, and funny. But when I let her see the weaker sides of me—insecure, wounded, and sad—I was rejected. It only reinforced what I had believed all along. In order to be accepted, I must concentrate on making others happy, deny my needs, and be happy-go-lucky so as not to cause any trouble.

I couldn't disagree with Heather. She wasn't able to bear all her burdens and mine too. I did need more than she had to give. Maybe my need of a friend for the journey wasn't wrong, but she didn't want to be that person anymore. I didn't blame her. She needed to take care of her own emotional well-being and that of her family. She was not responsible to see me through this tumultuous season of my life.

I understood all this with my head, but my heart was broken.

I must have asked God a million times: *Then why did I even meet her? What was the point of opening my heart to let somebody in, only to be hurt again? Things were going along just fine when I didn't care deeply. I don't want to depend on anybody but myself. It isn't worth it.*

The thing is, meeting Heather was worth it. The experience was ultimately about so much more than a broken friendship. It was about a broken heart, and brokenness was a necessary step to experiencing intimacy with God, myself, and others.

I was learning this in many of the books I was reading:

Brokenheartedness is related to spiritual poverty. It is the state of being wounded or crushed by some loss, person, hurt, injustice, or circumstance. When a person is downcast because of an emotional, relational, or career injury, he can be brokenhearted. God has special tenderness for this condition. Brokenheartedness often brings about a sense of our spiritual poverty as it shows us our need.[1]

"To know the love of Christ which surpasses knowledge," as Paul says in Ephesians 3:19 (NASB), was truly my deepest heart's desire. God was taking me along an age-old path to get there: acknowledging need, dependency, a broken heart, grief, awareness of sin, and inability of self-sufficiency to reconcile with God.

It helped a little once I could see what God was up to. I thought, "What a gentle God we serve. There were so many ways I could have experienced a broken heart: the death of a loved one, divorce, a terminal illness. Instead, he chose to give me a friend, allow me to experience heart closeness, and then take her away." I could say with conviction "The LORD gave, and the LORD has taken away; blessed be the name of the LORD" (Job 1:21, ESV).

Sorting It All Out

Not that I didn't grieve the loss. I did. Thankfully, I discovered a wonderful book to guide me through the different stages of grief. One of the things I loved the most about Walter Wangerin Jr.'s book *Mourning into Dancing* is that he helped me understand that grieving is about so much more than the death of a loved one. Grieving is the death or loss of anything of importance to your heart. One passage, in particular, felt like it was written just for me:

> And yesterday you had a friend, both necessary and near to you. This was one person with whom you experienced the fullness of your own individual life, because you revealed the whole of your soul to her: naked and unashamed, because she loved you and she honored you. You saved for her alone your secrets, your dreams

(however silly they might sound in any other ear), your memories of sweetness past, your hundred fears, your thousand weaknesses. With this friend there were no fig leaves, no clothing to cover the uttermost You.

I found it so helpful to read that as the friendship ends, a person will suffer. The friend and the friendship are gone, and you cry. However, he goes on to say:

> But immediately I tell you the kinder news: this is all normal. Don't think something like a poor diet or crummy weather caused your sorrow. Dear, you've suffered a significant death. The very arteries of your communal life were cut asunder. Trust was destroyed by her that was your friend, and lifeblood ran from the wound. You have a right to grieve."[2]

Wangerin refers to the breaking of communal relationships as Little Deaths. He gave me permission to feel the depth of my hurt when, otherwise, I was prone to feeling embarrassed that I was getting so worked up over the loss of a friend. Why couldn't I just get over it? He gave reason and weight to my loss as his book led me through the five stages of grief:

1. **Denial** (or shock). I can only remember grieving a handful of losses in my lifetime. The rest of them have

been buried deep beneath denial. I realized, as I was grieving the loss of this friendship, that I was, at the same time, grieving many other losses I could no longer even remember—consciously, that is. This wound was big enough to allow grieving but not so life-threatening that I felt the need to cut off my awareness of the pain. God, in his mercy, allowed me to feel the pain of loss and separation in a friendship that had barely taken root, while also tapping into the root system of very old separation losses.

2. **Anger.** I directed my anger toward myself. I must have rehearsed a million times all the mistakes I made. Of how I coulda/shoulda/woulda done it differently. I wrote a hundred letters in my head to her and had a hundred more conversations apologizing for my neediness and inability to accept what she was capable of offering. This was another childhood strategy. I determined early on that if the hurt I was feeling was caused by someone else then I had no control over the situation. If I took the blame and guilt then I could determine to learn from the situation, do better next time, and thus stay one step ahead of pain by being good enough.

3. **Bargaining.** Oh my goodness, I was a reading maniac. I read at least a book a day: books on friendship, healing, growth, spirituality, self-help, psychology, theology, commentaries, devotionals, biographies.

You name it, I read it. There was a desperate thirst in me to understand what went wrong, what was happening, what God was doing. I needed to believe that if I could wrap my mind around the pain then I could fix it and then stop it.

4. **Sadness.** The quieter voice inside knew that I couldn't make sense out of the suffering of this world, or my little world. When my louder conversations of denial, anger, and bargaining were drowned out by that truth, the soft sounds of sadness could be heard. That's when I retreated to my walk-in closet. I sat down on the floor by my shoes, pulled my knees to my chest, and allowed silent tears to stream down my face again. Before this picture sounds too dark, though, I must say that this is where the tender brilliance of God could shine the brightest. I thought the grief was about the death of a friendship—and it was. But, even more, it was about the death of my craving for control of my life.

5. **Acceptance.** I will write about this final stage now, but you must understand that all of these stages took a lot of time, and I didn't get to acceptance until months and months later.

There is no way around the time it takes to work through the stages of grief. I hated that fact! Being a strong woman from the South, I wanted to "get 'er done."

I wasn't ready to let go of my works for God's grace. I

still wanted to work hard, even as a griever. I wasn't able to receive the gift of resurrection yet. I didn't need anybody. It would be closer to the truth to say that I didn't want anybody to see me grieving. I didn't need pity. Besides, I was still having a really hard time trusting my vulnerable places with another person. Couldn't I just retreat to my closet, have a good cry with God, and then come out and have it all together again? Uh . . . no. That's just not the way we were created.

The first doctor I saw when I went away to the counseling center was the staff psychiatrist, and he knew this principle to be true. He determined that even though I had been crying for months, I wasn't clinically depressed and didn't need medications. He called my flood of tears situational depression, a healthy processing of grief. The kind and understanding man said, "I'm going to write you a prescription for a fireside chat. What you need is a friend to talk through everything that comes up so you don't have to carry your pain alone anymore."

Heather made it clear she didn't want to talk to me anymore, so I turned to the only person I knew who might understand. Through a mutual friend, I had recently met someone who was involved in a twelve-step recovery program. I knew if anyone could help me process my journey, this person could. There was only one minor problem.

This friend was a man.

Five

Where Do I Begin?

*I*f you're at all familiar with Alcoholics Anonymous, then you know that a person entering the group in an effort to break an addiction is assigned a sponsor. This is typically a person who has been where you have been in your addiction, is going where you want to go in your recovery, and knows how to get where you're headed on your journey.

That is the best way to describe who Craig became to me. Although I didn't suffer with an obvious addiction, I was definitely in recovery from addictive behavior in a variety of forms. Part of the reason for the success of the AA program is the sponsors. Craig was just what the doctor ordered.

Every day I would call and "check in" with Craig.

This consisted of just being honest about where I really was in that moment. Most days, I had trouble articulating how I felt. This is where Craig shined. He was a fabulous question-asker! I loved that he never gave me pat answers or instructions. He let me be where I was and then helped me find my own solutions . . . or not. It was okay to simply not know.

Some days I felt great, but mostly I felt blah. Secretly, I felt very embarrassed to be so heartbroken over an interrupted friendship. I first heard that phrase, interrupted friendship, when reading a book by Henri Nouwen called *The Inner Voice of Love*. Discovering it helped me not to feel like such a fool for my reaction.

Nouwen describes going to L'Arche, a faith-based community, and the process of opening his heart to others. One friendship in particular became important to him as no other ever had.

> But this deeply satisfying friendship became the road to my anguish because, soon, I discovered that the enormous space that had been opened for me could not be filled by the one who had opened it. I became possessive, needy, and dependent, and when the friendship finally had to be interrupted, I fell apart. I felt abandoned, rejected, and betrayed. Indeed, the extremes touched each other. Intellectually I knew that no human friendship could fulfill the deepest longing

of my heart. I knew that only God could give me what I desired. I knew that I had been set on a road where nobody could walk with me but Jesus. But all this knowledge didn't help me in my pain. Very old places of pain that had been hidden to me were opened up, and fearful experiences from my early years were brought to consciousness. The interruption of friendship forced me to enter the basement of my soul and look directly at what was hidden there, to choose, in the face of it all, not death but life. Thanks to my attentive and caring guides, I was able day by day to take very small steps.[1]

Craig was my attentive and caring guide, and every day he was there to hold my hand as I kept taking baby steps to walk through old pain by way of new pain. Anytime something came up in a present situation that caused me pain and tempted me to look elsewhere for relief, Craig would ask me, "What is beneath the longing?"

I learned to acknowledge and experience emotions that surfaced in everyday situations while internally asking myself questions: *When have I felt these same feelings in the past? Could they be an indicator of unresolved pain or unexpressed grief or unacknowledged yearnings?* I learned that my emotions were like the little warning lights in your car that come on to alert you to low tire pressure or an overheating radiator or the need for oil or fuel. How silly would

I look if I took my car into an auto repair shop and said, "The little lights in my dash are broken. The lights come on only occasionally and are extremely annoying. Please take the bulbs out so they won't bother me anymore."

Craig was teaching me to ask myself: *What is this emotion trying to tell me about something that needs attention under the hood?* Here's the catch, you can't just let anybody take a look under your hood. It needs to be somebody you really know and trust. After all, they are working with the powerful, yet sensitive, inner workings of your engine.

Perhaps you can see where I'm headed, or where Craig and I could have been headed if we weren't careful.

Did you know that the word *know* is the same word used in the original language of the Bible in Genesis 4:1 (NKJV), when the scriptures record that "Adam knew Eve his wife, and she conceived." I knew and trusted Craig and he knew me—in some ways better than my husband. But not in the biblical sense of the word! Nevertheless, there was an intimacy growing that was dangerous.

See, we are created body, soul, and spirit, all interconnected. It is very difficult to have a soul-to-soul connection with a man and not have your (and his!) body-to-body wires start firing. It's just the way we are built to run. I'm not saying it is impossible to know a man intimately at an emotional level and not desire physical intimacy. I'm just saying I started smelling the telltale odor of an electrical fire sparking, and I didn't want to play with it.

Nothing ever happened or even came close to happening. We lived in separate states, for starters; when we were in the same state, we never even shared a meal unless our spouses were with us. Nothing was ever mentioned or even hinted that we felt was inappropriate. I just know myself well enough to know that during my honest and vulnerable conversations with him, I was feeling drawn to him emotionally in a way that could easily cross the lines physically, if given the right circumstances. I've lived enough life to know that my best intentions are no match for the enemy's brilliant use of the weapons of deceit, moments of weakness, and things hidden.

I've also learned that any time I wonder if something is a work of darkness is a good time to test it to see if it stands up under the light.

So one day, I asked Craig, "Does your wife know that we talk every day?"

"She knows that we talk often," he said, "but I don't know if she knows it's a daily conversation."

I pressed a little further. "How do you think she would feel if she knew the frequency?"

"I don't know," he answered.

"I think it may be a good idea for you to ask her if she feels comfortable with the regularity of our phone calls," I suggested.

He called me the next day and explained that his wife had been feeling increasingly uncomfortable with our daily interaction and that he needed to honor her request that we not continue our friendship at this time.

I agreed wholeheartedly, and I have never had a private conversation with him since.

But I was back to square one: Wanting a friend. Needing a friend. Finding a friend. Losing a friend.

Wasn't friendship supposed to be easier than this?

My Best Friend Forever

Proverbs 18:24 says, "There is a friend who sticks closer than a brother" (ESV). Thankfully, I knew this to be more than a refrigerator magnet. It may sound corny, but truly, my best friend has always been Jesus.

God says in Jeremiah 1:5: "Before I formed you in the womb I knew you, before you were born I set you apart." I somehow understood this from as early as I can remember. There is no natural explanation. I wasn't raised in a church-going home. But as a small child, barely able to read, I was given a large picture book of Bible stories; whenever I was afraid or lonely or sad, I would lie on my tummy across my bed, look at the pictures, and read the stories. I fell in love with the Jesus in my Bible storybook. I think that is when he first became my best friend. I turned to him even then for comfort. He became my refuge before I ever knew him as Savior.

Later (I don't recall my age, maybe first or second grade), my father was invited to a church revival service by a coworker. Our whole family went. From the moment I walked through those church doors, I started to cry. I sat in the pew weeping the whole night. I didn't know why, and I was so embarrassed, but I couldn't stop crying.

I understand now that the presence of the Lord was in that place. Jesus walked straight through the wall that was already in place around my heart and touched my pain with his healing love. At the age of ten, I walked down the aisle of a little church and asked Jesus: "Come into my heart, forgive my sins, and be my Lord." But even before that official invitation, Jesus had been snuggling up like a cat to the most frightened places of my soul with gentle companionship.

Throughout my years in Hollywood, Jesus was more real and present to me than any other person in my life. If I were to picture my isolated heart like a deserted island, then it has just been Jesus and me in there for years. Now when you spend that much time with someone, you become really close, and my friendship with Jesus has been constantly growing in depth and breadth from the beginning, maybe even from before the beginning.

So at ten years old, I started the habit of reading a chapter of the Bible every night before I went to bed. As a teenager, I learned the pleasure of getting up early every morning to just hang out with him to talk about my day and life. In my twenties, we began walking together in the mornings before I had to go to work. Once I had kids, Jesus and I had most of our best conversations in the minivan. A few years ago, I discovered Bible study curricula. As I mentioned earlier, this is how I met Beth Moore, the Bible study queen, and that brings me to the next chapter in my friendship journey.

No, I didn't become best buds with Beth, but the next friend God used in my life is also a Bible study author who knows Beth personally. So, taking into consideration the six degrees of separation, I think Beth and I are practically sisters.

Seriously, the woman I'm talking about is Jennifer Rothschild, a brilliant Bible teacher and speaker who also happens to be blind.

Walking by Faith into Friendship

I first met Jennifer briefly at a Christian Booksellers Convention but got to know her much better in 2001. My family and I took a yearlong road trip around the United States in an RV, visiting forty-four states and traveling more than fifty thousand miles to discover America and, even more importantly, each other. Along the way, I had a speaking engagement at the church Jennifer attends in Springfield, Missouri. Of course, I had no idea then how ten years later her spiritual reflections and very life would speak to me in the way of an intimate friend.

Shortly after returning home from the counseling center, I started digging into a new Bible study, one written by Jennifer, *Walking by Faith: Lessons Learned in the Dark.*

I was being deeply ministered to by her insights every morning as I made my way through the study workbook. Jennifer wrote about how as a blind woman she discovered that "learning to walk by faith is much like learning to walk in the dark."[2]

It was compelling to me how her description of a walk in physical darkness felt so similar to my own recently foggy journey of faith. I especially related to her descriptions of very real dependency needs, her fear and aversion to trusting others, and her subsequent struggle with an ongoing desire to live a life of independence:

You know what qualifies someone to guide? Sight! Let's face it, though. Just because people can see doesn't mean they're worthy of my trust. Trust is a choice I make and a risk I take. Why? Because otherwise I'd never go anywhere! The journey is worth the risk . . .

Many things create islands of people's lives. We all find ourselves in situations where we feel isolated from others because we think they cannot truly understand our circumstances. As a result, a feeling of loneliness descends, soul-loneliness. It makes me cry out to be connected to someone who understands without words or explanation.[3]

I totally got where she was coming from because, as a television personality, I have always felt an imposed isolation. Strangers automatically think they know me. After all, they have grown up with me in their living rooms and homes, so they feel like we've shared childhood together and, therefore, are old friends. But I don't know them—they are strangers to me. When a stranger gets too close to you, what do you do? You protect yourself, which is what I've always done. I've always tried to be friendly, understanding, and accommodating to those folks who want an autograph or want to ask me a question. But the wall goes up immediately to protect the parts of me that are the real me and not the character I played. It's an isolating place, just like what Jennifer described in her book about navigating blindly in a world of sighted people.

So when I came to week four of Jennifer's Bible study and she talked about the importance of tears—wow. The timing couldn't have been more perfect. I felt affirmed and understood as I read:

Sometimes life hurts! When it does, we must admit our pain. We must learn to cry, not only in the physical act of shedding tears but also in allowing ourselves honest, heartfelt responses of sorrow or grief when those are warranted . . . To experience the life of faith, we must abandon our pride and humbly admit our sorrow, pain, and needs. To be tenderly accepting of our own humanity allows us to cry out; when we do, we feel the strengthening hand of our Mighty God.[4]

I had grown tired of crying so much and wondered when I was going to finally get over this and move on. Jennifer's comforting words about tears touched my soul, and I just had to call and tell her how much she had been a friend to me during this trying season of my life—a friend who probably didn't even know it.

When Jennifer picked up the phone and I started sharing how much her Bible study had meant to me, I started crying. Again! Why couldn't I control the floodgates anymore? I wanted to be able to cry again, but I also wanted to have some kind of say as to when I would and wouldn't blubber all over the place.

Jennifer wasn't willing to let the conversation end with my blathering admiration. With gracious sensitivity, she asked, "Could you tell me a little bit about this season you're in and how specifically my writing has helped you on your journey?"

I shared a particular story she had written about, a

beautiful picture of God and his heart for me during this time of struggle and suffering. The morning I read it, I remember laying my head back against the couch and the tears running into my ears:

> Perhaps you remember a vivid scene from the 1992 Barcelona Olympics . . . A young British runner was prepared for the run of his life. Derek Redmond's lifelong dream was winning a gold medal in the 400-meter run. The gun sounded in his semifinal heat, and Derek was running well until a pulled hamstring sent him sprawling facedown on the track.
>
> Determined to finish the race, Derek somehow got to his feet and began to hop toward the finish line. An older man made his way down out of the stands. Showing the same determination as the injured runner, he pushed aside security guards to reach Derek. The spectators watched Jim Redmond throw his arms around his son Derek, supporting him until they crossed the finish line together. The onlookers were on their feet, weeping and cheering.
>
> Derek Redmond didn't win the gold medal, but he knew his father loved him too much to stay in the stands, watching him suffer. That's the kind of Heavenly Father we have . . . a Father who loves us too much to stay out of reach when we struggle and suffer.[5]

Jennifer probed respectfully, yet persistently, "What do you think God is trying to say to you through all of this, Lisa?"

"Well, I'm zero-for-two in the close friend department," I joked, "but I still believe that God is asking me to be open to experiencing his love and touch through the heart and hands of the body of Christ, not just Jesus and his Spirit. That he is not content to stay on the sidelines and watch; that he will be there for me to lean on, but he also wants me to learn to lean on others for support when I'm weak and hurting."

The next thing she said brought me to tears. (I'm sure that surprises you, right?) She said, without hesitation, "Well, my friend, I'll walk this journey with you."

"Really?" I was astounded. *How cool that would be!* Strangely, I already felt like Jennifer had been walking beside me every morning through her Bible study. I never dreamed it would be possible that she could do that with me in real life.

Our friendship grew mostly through e-mail. For some reason, I haven't been able to journal this journey I've been on. I don't know why, because I've really wanted to be able to process my thoughts and feelings on paper, but I've experienced some kind of strange internal restraint. I loved the outlet of sharing my thoughts and feelings with Jennifer by writing to her.

I don't know what made me save this particular e-mail

paragraph. It was probably because it was so characteristic of the kind of friend Jennifer was becoming to me. She replied to one of my outpourings of emotions and fear with the following response:

> Oh, my friend, you are safe. That you can count on. No matter how long our friendship lasts, no matter how deep or shallow it ebbs and flows . . . I will be faithful to never disclose what you've entrusted me with, and I will remain loyal to God through the way I befriend you. Just relax, cry for the right reasons, and keep your trust in God higher than your trust in people, and all will be well!

There were many things about Jennifer that make perfect sense of why God would connect us again at this blustery season of my life. For one thing, she has phenomenal boundaries. She knows who she is and who she's not. She didn't feel compelled to rescue me, she trusted God with that job. Yet I still felt incredibly cared about by her.

She also had a strong support system in place, so I didn't have to worry about being too needy. She had other resources to draw from if I were emotionally draining at times. Of course, she was always quick to assure me that I was only imagining being an energy leech. She assured me I didn't need to worry, that the tables would surely turn someday and I would have a chance to be there for her in the future.

I could experiment with discovering who I really was, not who I was supposed to be. She gave me room to be strong one minute, and a whiny baby one hour later. I could have all the answers in one conversation and be full of questions the next. I might call her five times in one day or disappear for one week.

On the occasional opportunities when Jennifer and I get to hang out together in person, I have learned how to walk beside her. I step up to her side, she takes hold of my elbow, and I lead her through the twists and turns and obstacles in our path. That is what she has been doing for me. She stands by my side, allows me to take hold of her for support, and she guides me through this dark and treacherous road of trust.

Jennifer understands that this is a unique period of growth I'm experiencing. This season doesn't define me, just like blindness doesn't define her. It is not who we are, it is what we are growing through. I was so grateful; I finally found a friend for the journey.

Now, where could I find some more friends before I overburdened this one with my needs like I did the last one?

Six

New Friendships
with Old Friends

I hope I haven't given the impression that I didn't
have any friends. Ironically, I had lots of wonderful friends. I just wasn't what I would call *soul
close* to them. That's what I needed and wanted. Thankfully,
I soon discovered that this wasn't such a huge leap to make,
especially with friends I'd known for many years.

Because my wall was already beginning to come down,
the dynamics in my current friendships changed without
my being able to help it. By that, I mean I couldn't control
the change, nor did I have to try to make it happen. I was
different, and, therefore, my relationships were morphing
right before my very eyes—my very teary eyes. For instance,

this is how one of my oldest friends, Michele, described the shift in a recent e-mail to me:

> Dear Lisa,
>
> I realized something changed when the ordinarily effervescent Lisa was so burdened with grief that you could hardly get ready for an interview that was going to take place in a matter of minutes at your home in Texas.
>
> For twenty-plus years you never skipped a beat, and on this day, clearly the beat was irregular. You reached out and hugged me in a desperate gesture to explain your inability to compose yourself. Those days were gone. Whatever was happening was no longer on the back burner, but up-front and center.
>
> I recognized the behavior as a symptom of being taken on a once-in-a-lifetime trip, on the truth train. It is as if the universe gets tired of the mold that one makes for oneself, and breaks it. Thus leaving the individual with no mold and therefore requiring that individual to deal with what is on the inside because there is no longer a reliable structure for the outside to exist alone. Lisa, from that moment on, you became real to me.
>
> Love,
>
> Michele

Experiencing deep friendship was at the top of my priority list during my sabbatical. So I cashed in some of

my airline reward miles and made a trip to Los Angeles visit my old Good Medicine Club friends. For years, I had hosted this handful of girlfriends in my home to play games, eat girlie food, and commiserate on parenting chal- lenges. We had history together.

Maybe that is why the shift in our relationship hap- pened so easily over one long, wonderful lunch. We hadn't all been seated around the table together since I moved to Texas. It was just like old times . . . only it wasn't because I was not the same, and my friends sensed that immediately.

For one thing, we hadn't been talking more than fif- teen minutes before tears began to roll down my cheeks. Second, my friends were used to me asking questions, and I was usually the first one to begin, "So, tell me, what brings you a pocket of pleasure in the middle of these stressful days?" Or, "Can you share with me what you think about when you can't sleep at night?" I'd ask ques- tions designed to draw out their hearts and allow me to really see them and love them. I truly enjoyed this. I guess I've always been the designated interviewer because this came naturally to me. I always loved getting to know peo- ple, and I mean really getting to really *know* them, not just *about* them.

But I realize now that this is probably one of the rea- sons why my friends could never put their finger on why they didn't feel close to me. I always was interested in them, but my interest, interviewing, and listening were

81

also defense mechanisms to avoid opening up my own heart or need or vulnerability to receive.

So my friends were surprised when I suddenly not only had my own questions and doubts but also voiced them. And what was with me suddenly being vulnerable with my hurts and fears and uncertainties? This was an all-new situation, and an amazing thing happened when I began to let others inside my heart for the first time. They threw wide open the gates on their own hearts, and they invited me into the deepest recesses where their own questions and secrets were stored.

I was the one then surprised: *So this is what it feels like to be interdependent!* Why had I been scared of this for so long? It was exhilarating.

After moving to Texas, I had started another Good Medicine Club and called this one MomTime. In the beginning, MomTime was fashioned very similarly to my former group in California with lots of games, laughter, conversations about husbands and kids, and always something sweet to eat. But instead of once-a-week, we met the first Monday night of each month so the dads could keep the little ones. This gathering of friends was the perfect incubator to nurture the birth of the new, naked, needy, teary side of the old, protected, strong, laughing Lisa.

The first order of business was to change the agenda

from playing games to being real. Don't get me wrong, I still love to play board games, but I also wanted to make sure there was time for rich conversation.

Now, for most months, I have a conversation prompt already prepared before the girls arrive. For example, one of our most enlightening evenings happened when I asked each friend to describe her mother in just five words with a combination of both positive and negative aspects. Oh my! We talked until after midnight and I learned more about these friends than I ever could have if we had stuck to the typical girlfriend topics like kids, shopping, diets, and daily tasks and stresses. This time I was careful to open up, too, even going first to answer and open my heart.

Last month, one of the girls arrived having missed the prior meeting and had lost almost thirty pounds since we had seen her last. She explained that she had recognized that she was addicted to sugar. She realized that she couldn't eat it in moderation because it had become a drug to her. This started another after-midnight conversation as we all went around the table sharing our go-to addictions.

By the end of the night, and after many tears and much self-revelation, I felt closer to these women than I ever had before. I can only imagine that it would be so much easier to let go of our unhealthy attachments if we could experience this kind of holy communion among safe friends.

Hidden Treasures

When I moved back to Texas after living in California for twenty-eight years, I didn't have a chance to make many new friends at first. It is so much harder to meet new women when your kids are older and there aren't as many activities in which to mingle. All three of my children were in junior high—you know, that age when the last thing they want is to hang around Mom.

Thankfully, I did have my handful of MomTime friends. These girlfriends were all decidedly younger than I was and had small children, so it was also a wonderful mentoring opportunity for me.

My counselor agreed and encouraged me to practice being more transparent, vulnerable, and open to receiving, rather than reverting to old patterns. This felt extremely uncomfortable. At first I told myself I had really good, godly reasons for my defense mechanisms. *Who wants a weak leader?* I reasoned. *Women need strong, older women to look up to. If I'm vulnerable about some of my doubts and hurts, they might feel like they can't lean on me during their hard times, or think I don't really believe the promises I share with them from Scripture.*

Worse (and I'm embarrassed to confess this), it had never crossed my mind that I could receive from these young women just as much (maybe more!) as they could ever get from me. I was so intent on ministering to them as an older, wiser mom with hindsight and experience that I almost missed the possibility that they might have something to offer to me.

Also, I still had been looking, mistakenly, for that one perfect friend who would embody everything my soul longed for in a friendship on earth. God is so much more expansive and creative than that. Together my MomTime friends provided a bounty of friendship that was more than enough to meet my relational needs, without my looking to one single person to be what God alone can be.

Oh my, the treasure chest I've almost missed opening, though! Each woman in my MomTime group has given me so much out of her trove of uniqueness. I see the wisdom of God in calling us the "body of Christ." He could have called us his heart or his hands or his mouth. But, no, he knows we need every part of the body to be healthy. This wholeness and interdependence with a variety of friends is also what guarantees healthier relationships.

For instance, Amy has shown me what it feels like to have a friend who *makes* time for you. I don't think I'm the only one who has felt like everyone is too busy for friendship. I am constantly worried about calling anyone for fear of interrupting them or of bothering a friend if I need them to pick up my kids or help me in some way. With Amy, I know that she will move heaven and earth to be with me. I wonder if she knows what it does to a soul to have a friend who wants to be with you enough to slow down and make connection a priority.

Allison is a young pastor's wife from a neighboring church. I think we have offered each other an environment to be offstage. You see, so often people in ministry are expected to be perfect. How nice, then, to be perfectly imperfect and allowed to be human. Allison also knows the critical importance of keeping confidences: what happens at MomTime, stays at MomTime.

Kristi oozes empathy. She overflows emotion. If you're crying, she's crying. If you're successful, she's applauding. If you make a stupid joke, she laughs heartily like you are the funniest comedienne on earth. I am learning to open up and receive such a luxury of love and acceptance.

Sarah and Bridget have modeled what a healthy BFF bond looks like. They have been friends for more than ten years, talk every day, and carry each other's burdens with humor and practical support. They are there for each other. They were the first ones I told about my broken friendship, and they rushed in with understanding and care.

When Missi first joined our MomTime group, she didn't know the Lord in a personal way. She lived in the Bible Belt, but she wasn't from a church-going family and couldn't speak Christianese. What a blessing that alone was! Missi taught me that authenticity around the lunch table spoke louder than truisms even if they were true. From my own personal experience with Missi, being willing to be slightly earthy and radically real did more to invite her to church than the flying angels at the Christmas cantata.

All of these friends have taught me in their own way that we can minister just by being who we are. We don't have to *do* ministry to be used by the Lord in someone's life. Just ask me. I have been deeply blessed by the gift of each personality.

Not All Friendships Should Be the Same

I also concentrated on making new friends. Sure, it felt risky, but not for long. I soon learned that most women were longing for friendship and welcomed the invitation. Since I was still on my sabbatical, I had time to reach out to women I knew, or had met, or just wanted to know, and I could invite them to meet me for lunch or coffee or a walk around the neighborhood. I was soaking it all in and getting filled up.

Of course, I understand that I was in a very unique situation, having taken a year off from writing to concentrate on friendships. I know that relationships are harder to cultivate in some seasons and even more difficult to sustain in others. Between kids, work, exhaustion, schedules, and simply not valuing ourselves enough to make time for friendships, it can feel next to impossible.

Then again, not all relationships have to be the same.

I like the way Jesus had three *really close* friends, a dozen *close* friends, and a larger circle of just *friend* friends.

In my own life, Nancy McKeon, who played the character Jo on *The Facts of Life*, is one of my *really close* friends. I have known her for more than thirty years. We grew up together. We shared life-shaping experiences. We get each other like only a handful of people on this planet could understand. She knew me when I was a squirrely teenager and when I suffered my first broken heart. We took turns dipping chocolate Hershey's Kisses in jars of peanut butter while the other stayed on guard to make sure none of our producers were watching. We shared a condo after she moved away from home. I can tell Nancy anything, and I know she won't judge me or stop loving me. We don't see each other often, but if I made a new friend now, I would be in my late seventies before I could have the kind of history with that woman like I do with Nancy.

In my next circle of friendship is my friend Michelle Smith. I wouldn't say we have as intimate a friendship as I have with Nancy, but she definitely is one of my *close* friends. We are close enough that she could say without hurting my feelings, "Are you really going out in public wearing that?" Michelle doesn't live near me, but at least twice a year we meet to catch up and go shopping. I hate shopping, and my wardrobe reflects my disdain. But Michelle cleans out my closet of comfy clothes and dresses me in the latest fashions. I don't know what I'd do without her.

She also knows how to cheer up a friend who is heart-broken. As God would have it, I happened to be with Michelle on the day after one of my lowest days on this journey. God knew who would know just what to do. For Christmas, her sweet husband gave her a gift certificate for a day of pampering. Michelle signed it over to me, took me to the day spa, and ordered up just what a girlie-girl like Michelle would know would make me feel better.

And then there is my circle of good, old *friend* friends. These are mostly people at my church and people I work with occasionally. I like being with them, but I don't go out of my way to stay connected to them. That is one thing I've learned: If you don't intentionally nurture your friend-ships and invest time in them, then they too easily dwindle away in the press of life.

I've never been much of a phone talker, but I've become one in order to stay in touch and connected with friends. I keep my circle of *really close* and *close* friends in my speed dial so that whenever I find myself in the car alone I can take advantage of that opportunity to reach out and say, "Hey, I'm thinking about you today." More often than not, I have to leave a message, but that's okay. The important thing is for me to let my friends know I care.

I know that kind of connection means the world to me. My friend Priscilla Shirer calls me almost every day. Most of our conversations are no longer than half a min-ute and are invariably cut short by a screaming baby or fighting youngster, but she reaches out, and it touches me.

With some friends, I know, if possible, to pull over to the side of the road of my day's agenda to take the call because if I don't "*carpe* the cell phone and seize the opportunity," I might miss it. I know this about my friend Angela Thomas. Her life has been so busy as a single mother that the only time she has to connect is if she is on a road trip in between speaking engagements. We may not talk for months, but if we talk as fast as we can then we can almost get all caught up at these in-between times.

Given everyone's schedules and responsibilities, mercy and grace are a prerequisite for modern friendships. Here is an e-mail I sent to my friend Jennifer early on in our relationship when we were trying to find a balance between life and anything else:

Dear Jenn,

Let me just say a quickie thank you for your quickie e-mail. I think one of the things we busy women (well, when I used to be busy) tend to do is not respond at all until we have time for a long conversation or thorough e-mail response. I do think part of what we can learn in this friendship that will probably take trial and error and honesty and mercy is how to balance making time for the relationship because of its eternal value and yet not dismissing the reality that we have to do what we have to do.

I am grateful for your quick responses, but I will trust your heart and intentions when you can't give one. I hope we find more opportunities to talk on the phone, but I also love the kind of ease in a friendship that can call and the other person say, "I can't talk now; gotta go." Click. (On the other hand, if you don't like the Cloud and Townsend audiobook that I sent you then I'm afraid the friendship is over.)

Love, Lisa

Yes, friendships take time, but if we wait until we have time for them then we'll never have them. I like the way my friend Anita Renfroe describes it. "Friends are like little chicks," she says. "When they are new, they need to be in the incubator and coddled over with lots of time and attention, or they'll never grow. After they get a bit older, they can survive in less than perfect conditions."

I first met Anita at a women's event where we were both speaking. After I spoke and walked off the stage, she ran straight up to me and said, "You are my new best friend!"

We actually did become instant friends by spending the evening talking into the night. A few months later, she was traveling to Dallas with Women of Faith, and she invited me to go with her. I had no idea my life was about to change in a million different ways.

Seven

Women of Faith

he first time I attended a Women of Faith event, I was more than excited. For years, I had wanted to attend, but I was always out of town speaking on the weekend they came to Dallas. I was especially thrilled to attend the "Friday Feature" because I was going to get to hear Dr. Henry Cloud speak—and I've read all his books. In fact, his teaching has been foundational for me, so I was ready to hang on his every word.

Who knew that not just what came from onstage but also from backstage would it affect me so? I certainly didn't, but I have since thought that my first Women of Faith weekend was like something Edith Schaeffer said:

The thing about real life is that important events don't announce themselves. Trumpets don't blow, drums don't beat to let you know you are going to meet the most important person you've ever met, or read the most important thing you are ever going to read, or have the most important conversation you are ever going to have, or spend the most important week you are ever going to spend. Usually something that is going to change your whole life is a memory before you can stop and be impressed about it. You don't usually have a chance to get excited about that sort of thing . . . ahead of time![1]

Have you ever been in a meeting where it feels like everything spoken is meant just for you? That's what the day felt like for me. At one point, Dr. Cloud talked about the obstacles to growth. He mentioned that we must beware that Satan is not going to give up on us easily because he has much invested in us staying stuck and being afraid to grow.

Dr. Cloud cautioned us to pay attention and realize that at the first sign of growth, Satan would surely jump in and sabotage whatever good was happening, that he had a vested interest in thwarting any progress we were making toward change. Specifically, Dr. Cloud told us to pay attention to times when we were learning how to relate in new ways rather than out of old, self-protective patterns.

I couldn't believe it when he used the illustration of finding a new friend and risking vulnerability and honesty, only to have that friend reject you as soon as you were beginning to trust. He challenged us not to slink back into our shell but instead take that as an indication that we were doing exactly the right thing. That's what scared the enemy enough to put the kibosh on our first attempt.

How did he know exactly what I had been through and what I was feeling?

All I wanted to do was give up and go back to my safe way of relating that made room for friendly relationships but kept enough space between me and everyone else to make sure no one ever got close enough to hurt me that deeply again.

But as I listened to him describe exactly what happened and how Satan was counting on me to give up, I felt a little fight rise up within me. I prayed silently: *Okay, Lord, I am willing to be open again, but next time around will you please send me a friend who has time in her life and space in her heart for me?*

Those trumpets Edith talked about could have been blaring just about then.

God Sends an Emmitt

During the last session, Dr. Cloud told a story about his mother going through an especially rough time in her life when he was a little boy. After he grew up, he asked her how she got through such a hard season that was obviously bigger than she could have endured on her own.

She simply replied, "Emmitt."

Dr. Cloud learned that Emmitt was his mother's best friend, and every day when his mother didn't think she could make it through another minute, she would call her friend, and Emmitt would simply hang on the phone and let her cry. Or Emmitt would say, "You do have the strength to do this," and then she would wait on the line while Dr. Cloud's mother went and did the next hard thing. Then Emmitt would say: "Call me tomorrow. Or call me in five minutes. I'm here for you whenever you need me."

As I listened to this story, I began to sob.

Anita was sitting beside me, so she put her arm around me and asked very gently, "Do you have an Emmitt?"

I bawled, "No, and I really need one."

She hesitated and then said, "Well, I would make a sucky Emmitt . . . but I will pray that God will send you an Emmitt."

Thank God for honest friends! How wise she was not to promise more than she could deliver. If she had responded out of her sympathy, I might have missed my Emmitt.

As it turns out, my Emmitt was in the same room while the tears of my longing flowed, but our paths weren't ordained to cross until the next afternoon.

During the last break on Saturday, I was sitting alone on the front row when the sweetest face I have ever seen stooped down and introduced herself. "My name is Ney Bailey," she said, "and my sisters and I are going to use the restroom backstage. I noticed that you were sitting alone, and if you need to go and would rather not fight the concourse rush, you are welcome to come with us."

I recognized the woman's name because earlier in the conference, one of the speakers told a story and mentioned her as "dear friend and 'Emmitt,' Ney Bailey."

Now I don't remember if I really had to use the bathroom then or not, but I accepted Ney's gracious invitation and was mesmerized by this most precious woman and both of her sisters, who were equally engaging.

As we headed back to our seats, I thanked Ney and said goodbye. Sitting alone again I felt like the little bird in that P. D. Eastman book, *Are You My Mother?* I kept sneaking a peek down the row, thinking, *Are you my Emmitt?*

Finally I wrote down my phone number and e-mail address and passed a note down the row that read, "I would love to get together with you for coffee or lunch sometime if that would be possible."

I don't know what possessed me to do that because it is so not like me. I couldn't believe I had let down my guard and invited in a stranger. But I guess when you get to a place where you know your need is great enough, you will risk a little embarrassment.

A few minutes later, a little note came back my way, this one with Ney's contact information.

I knew I had made some progress in the friendship department but I was still insecure. So a couple of weeks went by, and I lost the courage to call Ney.

I was talking one afternoon to Jennifer when I mentioned meeting Ney, and Jennifer was thrilled. Her voice went up an octave, and she said, "Oh, Lisa, if you have the opportunity to spend even five minutes with Ney Bailey, don't miss out. She is amazing. People affectionately refer to her as 'the fourth person of the Trinity.'"

So I sent Ney an e-mail and asked if she would have any time to meet with me.

Ney responded very graciously, and we set up lunch for the following week. Seated across the restaurant table from her felt like sitting in a cushion of love and grace. How could a stranger make me feel so at home almost instantly? I have since learned that every person who ever encounters Ney feels the same way—like you are the only person in the world at that moment, that your story is the most interesting one she's ever heard, that she is feeling your heartache with you, that God is speaking his words through the most beautiful voice.

I now know that Ney always prays before (or while) meeting someone: "Lord, may I be to them what they need in you. And only you know what that is."

Well, God certainly answered her prayer on this day. I didn't realize how much I needed someone to receive me. I always felt more comfortable giving. So, at first, it might sound contradictory to say that I needed someone to receive me. There is a subtle, yet huge, difference between giving *of* myself and giving my *very* self. I could give my service, my words of encouragement, my time, practical advice, a listening ear, and my prayers. But it felt an odd combination of becoming too vulnerable and being too selfish to open up and give someone my very self—me and only me, not what I could do or say.

Ney created an atmosphere of acceptance and interest that drew out the me who no longer worried about how protected I could stay. She asked questions and then follow-up questions, and then I'd realize we were on a bunny trail talking about something I never would have imagined sharing out loud with someone. But I loved talking about me . . . and that was so unlike me.

Ney made me feel so valuable. After I told her about my disappointment over my recent broken friendship, she asked how I was feeling about it now.

After spending two hours with this most amazing woman who had the uncanny ability to affirm me by her eyes and smile and ears, I still can't believe how I answered her question. "Heather said that I was too heavy," I answered. "Now, I'm thinking, maybe I was too heavy, like a pot of gold is heavy. Now I'm thinking she missed out."

Ney grinned. "I'm so glad to hear you say that," she said. "That tells me that even in the midst of rejection, you know you are valuable. You are worth what was given for you. God gave Jesus for you, and you are worth that much to him." This is the kind of gift Ney possesses. In her presence, you feel a reflection of how God must feel about you.

We tried to make plans to meet again soon, but my speaking schedule was crazy the following month, so we had to wait. That's when we started talking by e-mail. The biggest blessing that came from this was the surprise discovery that she was somehow able to receive me even more perceptibly via e-mail.

I would send an e-mail to her before I went to bed, telling her all about my day. When I woke up in the morning, I would rush to my computer (even before the coffeepot) so I could read her reply. She would take each paragraph and respond to it. Is it just me, or is this the sweetest of gifts: for someone to put so much value on your life and what you have to say that they will take the time to receive your words and offerings and then respond to each one of them personally and uniquely?

For goodness sakes, we live in Facebook and Twitter times where we communicate in 140 characters or less. I am part of both of these social networks, but it is so easy to think we are staying in touch with friends this way when, in reality, the touch is often while we are simply brushing by them as we are rushing through our busy lives that are too crowded for meaningful contact.

At this point, I hadn't ever called Ney on the phone.

That felt too pushy or presumptuous or close or something. But while I was in Florida on a speaking trip, I felt a heaviness that didn't make sense. It wasn't about anything in particular, but I wasn't able to pray or praise it away either.

I held my breath and called Ney. I was anxious. Reaching out, admitting my need, and asking for help was still a scary proposition. Ney answered in her gracious, endearing way, and shared a couple of meaningful scriptures off the top of her heart, ready to comfort and encourage. Most of all, she just listened to me and responded with empathetic sounds.

When I went back to the hotel that night, I prayed: "Oh Lord, I feel so inadequate to be Ney's friend. I don't feel like I have much to offer to her in comparison to what she has already given to me in this short time since I've met her. Would you please show me how I can pray for her—at least I can give her my prayers, and then you can give to her through other means what I don't have to offer."

That night, I dreamed that I was seated way up in the bleachers of a stadium, watching a football game. I was cheering on the whole team, but my eyes were glued to one player in particular. (I found out the next morning that the position was called an offensive lineman.) All I knew was that every time the ball was moved down the field, this player took hard hits while making it possible for the other team members to make the plays and eventually score the touchdowns.

My heart went out to this player, and I ran down to the sidelines to tell him to get off the field or he was going to get really hurt! The football player reached up and took off his helmet . . . only it wasn't a "him." It was Ney!

"Thank you for your empathy," she said in my dream, "but I'm a big girl and I've chosen this position. I will be fine. Don't worry about me."

When I woke up, I couldn't believe God had answered my prayer so quickly and clearly. I could see that Ney is very much an offensive lineman in these, her latter years of ministry. Because of her team-player mentality, she is more than content to run interference for the many people in her life who are on the front lines of ministry. Ney does this through prayer and practical support—mostly through her gift of friendship.

I understood through that dream that the best thing I could do for Ney was to see her. So many of the eyes in that stadium were on the playmakers. My eyes were to be on her, looking out for her, caring for her, while she did her job of taking care of others. I could do that! I thanked God for the privilege.

Giving and Receiving

From the beginning, I had wondered what in the world I could ever offer this incredible woman for there to be any kind of healthy reciprocity in our relationship. During our second lunch, Ney assured me, "I'm not worried about that. I know the way God works. Whenever he is working on one side, he is also working on the other. I will be blessed by you too."

The next day I sent her the following text message:

How grateful to the Lord I am for the sweet, tender, valuable gift of your friendship. He must love me an awful lot to send you to me. Praying for a peaceful, happy, healthy day for you.

Love,

Lisa

I didn't know she didn't know how to text! She was in the doctor's office when her phone beeped. Thankfully, there was a nurse who helped her read it and send out a short reply. Now, she's a text-messaging hound dog! I guess she was right. I was able to bless her life in a tangible way. I brought her into the twenty-first century of technology. I don't know what kind of jewels I'll get in my crown in heaven for that, but it's at least something.

The next day, Ney left on an unplanned trip. There had been a tragedy in her family, and she rushed off for the funeral and to comfort her loved ones. While she was away, she was able to receive text messages but hadn't gotten the hang of sending them, which gave me the perfect opportunity to give a little something back to her. I sent her texts of encouragement and prayer throughout her difficult days.

God truly was working on both sides now.

Later I would learn that Ney, like me, felt more comfortable in the giving role. But by God's orchestrating circumstances in such a way that she was not able to give—she had to simply receive—he was healing her heart too.

We were also alike in that it was a big step for her to reach out for help. While she was away, a spider bit her, and the bite wasn't healing even after she returned home. In a bold move, she figured out texting enough to send me a message asking me to pray for her while she was in the doctor's office. What a simple thing to request, and yet I so understood her reluctance to risk asking.

What has conditioned so many of us to be afraid to ask for help when we need it? Or to reach out for a touch when we are lonely? Or to forgo sharing a happy success for fear of sounding prideful? Why do we choose the safety of space in even the closest of friendships?

I am realizing that it isn't just me who feels wobbly and insecure taking my first steps toward grown-up friendships. Even saints, who have walked in godly relationships their whole lives, sometimes feel afraid of taking awkward steps toward others.

Journaling the Journey

It was now Christmas, and over the holidays, Ney went for a lifetime adventure to Rome with four friends she's known for more than thirty-five years. While she was out of the country, I continued to write her an e-mail every night, even though I didn't send them.

I had always wanted to keep a daily journal, but I stink at it, so this was as close as I'd ever come to doing so. It seems as if I had started countless daily journals too many Januarys, and never made it past February in actually keeping one. How fun it was to discover finally the joys of writing to a friend every night. I enjoyed writing out for Ney all the goings on of my day, and the ins and outs of my heart. I was journaling!

I also was growing in a way I hadn't anticipated. By expressing my thoughts and exposing my heart before another human being, I was learning about myself through the reflection in another's eyes. My daily writings became like a diary and a mirror all in one. Sharing my life with another person on paper was so much more fun than actually keeping a journal just because I knew it was a spiritual discipline that was good for me—kind of like the yummy, pink liquid antibiotic I used to give my kids when they had an ear infection. The medicine was so delicious the kids didn't even know they were taking something good for them, something that would even eventually stop the pain.

Keeping in touch with each other's lives through e-mail is especially helpful during busy seasons of life, whether it is when our work schedules are especially heavy or when our kids are small and we are too exhausted to put two words together at the end of the day. I was grateful for the opportunity to stay in contact with Ney while she was away and before that while I was coming and going with so many ministry travels. As Henry Cloud writes:

> God made us to need Him and each other. We need God. We need his Word. We need each other. The apostle John wrote, "I have much to write to you, but I do not want to use paper and ink. Instead, I hope to visit you and talk with you face to face, so that our joy may be complete" (2 John 12). Complete your own joy. Come face to face with others who love you.[2]

So, after the first of the year, I asked Ney if we could meet once a week instead of every month. We decided to meet for lunch every Tuesday, like Mitch and Morrie in the book *Tuesdays with Morrie*. I usually came with a Post-it note full of bullet point things I wanted to make sure we didn't forget to discuss. Oftentimes we would share our "underlinings," thoughts about a book we both were reading, what we liked or didn't, what was meaningful. Always, we'd wrap up our time by praying together for the week ahead and the cares of our hearts.

As you've probably already surmised, Henry Cloud is one of my favorite authors. In yet another one of God's divine (ahem) coincidences, it turns out that Ney has known Henry for years and has integrated into her life much of what she's learned from him. She's had the opportunity of benefiting from his wise counsel since his earliest years as a psychologist. She even said to him early on, "Mark my words, Henry. The world is going to hear from you someday."

She wasn't wrong. Henry Cloud has written more than twenty books and inspired millions with his beautiful blending of psychology and theology. I've been more influenced by his books than by any of the hundreds of others I've read. Isn't it just like the Lord to send me a friend who could teach me firsthand what she had been taught by a master?

As Ney predicted, our friendship has become mutually beneficial. Even though I am a former actress in my forties and she is a former missionary in her seventies, we are kindred spirits.

God really was working on both sides when he caused our paths to cross at that Women of Faith event. Since then, Ney has taught me about "conversational prayer," and I've taught her about worship. She's tutored me in conflict resolution, and I've kept her computer running. She has given me classic books, and I've supplied her with a never-ending flow of new ones to read. Much of what I write in the rest of this book was born out of experience or in conversation with "my Emmitt, Ney."

What I didn't know when I first met Ney was that she has been friends with Mary Graham, the president of Women of Faith, for more than thirty-five years. I guess you could say that I joined The Porch Pals by The Back Porch gals first.

Life on The Porch

As anyone who has ever attended a Women of Faith event probably already knows, The Porch Pals are Patsy Clairmont, Marilyn Meberg, Luci Swindoll, and Sheila Walsh. These women have spoken on the team from the beginning and are still going strong. What you may not know is that in addition to The Porch where the speakers and artists sit connected to the stage, there is also a Back Porch. It is located just to the right of The Porch and is the hub of all the inner workings, and at the heart of it all is Mary Graham. This is also where Ney was sitting the day I met her and where I was sitting as an invited guest of Anita Renfroe.

This is a perfect picture to illustrate how I was invited onto The Porch. I came in through The Back Porch and entered through the back door. Through Ney, I became friends with Mary and eventually with Luci, Marilyn, Sheila, and Patsy.

One afternoon, I was at a birthday party for Mary's sweet niece, Ruth Ann, when Marilyn blurted out, "Lisa, you do what we do. Why don't you do it with us?" Little did I know, Mary had already been mulling this idea over with her team of vice presidents, and I soon received a phone call to begin the process of joining The Porch Pals.

I was beyond excited.

Just this morning, I did a phone interview, and the reporter asked me how it felt to be a part of the Women of Faith team. I explained that I have felt a deep sense of calling to use whatever platform God has given me to tell as many people as possible about his love for them. I've traveled and spoken at events for over thirty years. For me, being invited to speak at Women of Faith is like being a baseball player and getting the opportunity to play in the World Series—a huge privilege.

As I continued to share for the newspaper article, I realized that honor paled in comparison to the blessing of spending time with such incredible women in such a close environment.

Ney once told me, "Lisa, until you embarked on your journey and learned about grace, you weren't ready to join Women of Faith."

After having spent hours with each of these women, I understand more of what she was trying to say. Each of

The Porch Pals has known grace at an experiential level and not simply in theory or theology. There is an authenticity that is born out of suffering and hope, which creates a safe place for women to come just like they are into the arena each weekend to receive the unconditional love of God.

Looking back, only God could have answered a prayer like this—and so exceedingly, abundantly above anything I could have imagined. A relatively short time ago, I desperately needed friends. Who knew the most wonderful friends a girl could ever ask for were waiting just around the corner to welcome me with an embrace of grace. He knew.

God is no respecter of persons. Remember, I went decades without close friends, mostly because I didn't even know I needed them and I certainly wasn't emotionally ready to receive them. This has been a long, hard journey, but he has abundant surprises waiting along the way—for me and for you too.

One of the first things I noticed about these women was how sincerely supportive and intimately invested they were with each other. I soon recognized that this flowed down from the headwaters of Mary Graham. She is the ultimate cheerleader. Whether she is effusively Tweeting her love and admiration for the people in her life or going out of her way to notice and build up a volunteer backstage, she is the definition of encourager. Everyone on her team is like this. I want to be like them.

I believe this is the secret of the depth of friendship

among The Porch Pals. They have traveled together for more than a dozen years. They have stood alongside one another while ministering to more than four million women during this time. They have held hands and hearts through deaths and births, harvests and deserts, and lived real life on and off the platform. Somehow, they are able to focus on the truth of the goodness of God without denying the sadness of the world around us. Besides authenticity, the most pervasive quality I have experienced with these women is encouragement. I have learned a lot about true friendship by hanging out with them.

For example, early on, I remember watching Marilyn hop onto a hotel shuttle after an event. On her way to sit down, she singled out two or three people to speak a uniquely personal word of encouragement that, underneath the compliment, also said, "I saw you. I affirm you. You are worth noticing. I like you."

Then she sat down next to me, skipped the niceties, and went straight to the heart of the matter, "Dear Lisa, how are you feeling in your soul?" We proceeded to have a deeply connecting conversation in the less-than-fifteen-minute journey to our destination.

I thought to myself, *Now that is how deep friendships are made*.

My first encounter with Patsy was through tears in the green room. It was my first weekend with them, and I felt like I had failed miserably. I so wanted to do a good job for them. I still equated love and acceptance with being good and performing well. I hadn't measured up to the standard I had set for myself, and I was distraught. This was about more than doing my job, and, I confess, this wasn't about performing for an audience of One either. I knew God loved me, but I wanted these women to like me. I thought that meant I needed to earn their approval by impressing them with my speaking skills. It was all I could do not to run out of that arena. I didn't feel like I deserved to be there, and I felt way in over my head.

I was choking back tears when Patsy pulled up a chair beside me and spoke with such insight and understanding: "I know how you feel because I have been there myself a million times. The standard we set for ourselves is perfection, and that is never attainable, and then we beat ourselves up when we fall short. You don't have to be perfect. Just be you. God called you to this position, and he knew who you were and what you had to offer that no one else could when he chose you. He believes you can do this. Can you rest in his faith in you?"

This is a hard concept to grasp: that I am okay, just the way I am, without being someone I'm not. Maybe that is one of the reasons God has allowed me to spend time with Luci Swindoll. She lives and breathes acceptance, first of herself and then out of that peaceful place, acceptance of others.

I love to learn from Luci, and she loves to teach. I have

been an actress since I was in the sixth grade, and that is the last year of formal education I received. Through tutors on the set and a homeschool curriculum, I graduated from high school, but in reality everything of importance I have learned through books, travel, and experience. Luci has lived her whole life this way, so it was natural for us to want to share our adventures with each other. She is a trailblazer, and I am grateful for the opportunity to learn from such a vanguard.

Sheila is one of the funniest, tenderest, smartest women I've ever met. If that weren't enough, she is an incredible dresser! A few weekends ago, I was getting dressed right before catching the shuttle over to the arena on a Friday night. Minutes before I was to meet the other Porch Pals downstairs, I discovered that the shirt I was planning to wear hadn't made it into my suitcase. I quickly threw on the outfit I was planning to wear on Saturday.

While seated on The Porch that evening, I leaned over and confessed to Sheila, "I may have to wear this outfit again tomorrow. How embarrassing! I somehow managed to get out the door without all my clothes."

She jumped right in, "I brought some extra clothes; why don't you come to my room tonight and see if anything appeals to you?"

I was thrilled. I knew Sheila had the coolest clothes! (I won't even mention her shoe collection.)

That evening Sheila loaned me the most gorgeous

purple suede jacket and shirt to go with it. I put that together with the black pants I brought with me, and I was stylin'! Not only that, but the buckle on my black pants had recently broken, so I was keeping it together with black electrical tape. The shirt she let me borrow even covered the unsightly adhesive. Perfect.

The next day, I got so many compliments. Plus, the outfit was so much more comfortable than the one I had left back at home. I felt beautiful in it. Sheila really has a gift of fashion. She also has the gift of giving.

I woke up Sunday morning to a text message from her, telling me that she wanted me to keep the shirt and jacket. I immediately had two reactions: First, I can't accept this gorgeous jacket; second, I really want it! I texted her back my gracious refusal. She responded with the most tender reply:

Honestly Lisa, it would make me very happy for you to do this. It really was God's idea. I woke up with his words in my heart: "Give this to my little girl from me."

I was ecstatic and so deeply touched by both my friend and my Father. Clothes are not my strength. I hate shopping. It depresses me, and I'm not good at it. I feel fat and ugly in everything I try on, so I just give up and go see a movie.

I'm discovering that friends are good for just about all

113

that ails you. But they can't be just any kind of friends. They have to be safe friends.

Women of Faith has been a safe harbor as I continue to navigate the sometimes treacherous waters of friendships. A few overwhelming waves of relationship hurts have almost capsized me a few times. I know what it feels like to be hit by the tsunami of betrayal.

Eight

Who Are Safe People?

One of the most critical lessons in friendship is learning to identify safe people. I, unfortunately, learned this the hard way. The moment my heart began to open up, I wanted to let everyone in. Because I had so little real life experience with friendships, I didn't know you had to be careful who had access to the deepest recesses. The first woman I opened my heart to was Heather. The second one was Lauren. Apparently, the plan was to knock me out with a one-two punch.

I loved Lauren! She was so real and vulnerable, and she invited me to be real and vulnerable too. She had embarked on the truth train a few years ahead of me, and she was still chugging along, sometimes derailing but always getting back on track and bravely letting the Engineer determine the direction and speed of her journey.

I admired and applauded the growth I witnessed in her. She had been through some rough stuff in her childhood and God was doing a deep emotional healing, but it hadn't happened without significant pain and endurance. She was a role model to me of what God could do if we were willing to trust him to do open-heart surgery, sometimes without anesthesia.

One day Lauren came over to my house while her kids were with their father for the weekend. She began to share some very personal stories with me about traumatic things she had suffered in her first marriage. I was shocked at what she had endured, and her sharing of it made me love and respect her all the more. I felt so entrusted and honored that she would share such intimate secrets with me.

I was completely caught off guard, however, when she began asking me equally personal questions. I felt like a deer caught in the headlights. I didn't want to lie, but I also didn't feel comfortable telling some of my own very private issues with someone I was still getting to know. Lauren continued to ask direct questions, and although I'm great at denial, I'm not such a good liar; so I responded truthfully, offering up some intimate details.

By the time Lauren left my home, I felt exposed and uneasy, but I thought maybe this was part of learning to be more vulnerable and real with friends.

Over time, I felt more and more comfortable opening up hidden rooms of my heart and inviting Lauren in. I was grateful to have someone go with me into some of the dark and scary places of my life. She, in turn, continued to share some of her shame-filled memories. I held her confidences close to my heart and determined to keep such private details just that—private. I knew that I would never tell another soul her secrets, not even my husband; I assumed that since I felt that way, everyone else did too.

You can imagine my shock and embarrassment when I found out that Lauren had told several people things I never wanted anyone to know.

One evening, our mutual friend Heidi and I went to see a movie. After the show, when I pulled up to Heidi's house, she lingered in the car. I could tell she wanted to tell me something. Tears welled in her eyes.

I begged Heidi to share what was wrong. She finally got up the nerve to tell me that her friend Caitlyn had told her that Lauren had shared one of my deepest, darkest secrets. I felt like I had been socked in the stomach. My friend covered her eyes in shame for me. Feelings of hurt and gratefulness surged with that single gesture. I was devastated by my broken confidences but extremely thankful that Heidi cared enough to tell me what was going on behind my back.

I drove home stunned, walked into my house, and

crumbled in a heap of hurt and shame. My mind ticked off a laundry-list of all my doubts and fears:

Why did I dare trust? It wasn't worth it.

This is what happens when you open your heart to another person. It's foolish to trust.

It's stupid to be real.

I don't want to do this anymore. I want to go back to the time when life was easy and when it was hard it didn't matter because I couldn't feel it.

This is a dumb journey I'm on, and I feel double-crossed and betrayed by God even more than Lauren. Why would God do this to me?

I don't know how to do relationships!

I've failed at friendships, and I don't think I can bear to try again.

It's too hard, too unpredictable.

There is too much possibility for getting hurt again and again. Only an idiot would willingly open herself up to this kind of suffering.

After a few days of crying in my pillow and out to the Lord, I knew there was only one thing to do. I had to forgive Lauren. That didn't mean I had to forget her careless actions. It didn't even mean that I had to trust her again. I would never forget; I was hurt too deeply. Besides, I didn't want to forget the lesson I was learning about the place of wisdom and discernment in friendships.

I didn't know if I could ever trust her again, but I

would give her a chance to earn back my trust, if she so chose. The truth was hitting me that I didn't have a choice whether to forgive Lauren or not. I gave up that choice when I received God's forgiveness for all my sins. So I spewed out all my anger and hurt to God and then with the mercy he had given me, I sat down to write the following e-mail:

Dear Lauren,

We've hit a bump in our friendship, but I want to keep it in perspective. Over the last week or so, the Enemy has done his best to convince me that I have been a fool to risk intimate friendships. Daily, hourly, I have been tempted to run as fast as I can back to my safe place of self-protection. But I will not let him win. God has a promise waiting for me in the territory beyond this fear, and I will not run from the battle.

Sure, I will be more careful in the future before I open up so readily. That is simply wisdom. But as irony would have it, I will also be more full of care. Jesus said, "He who has been forgiven little loves little" [Luke 7:47].

I have been forgiven so much; and because of that I will love more, not less. I desperately need mercy and forgiveness in so many areas, for so many things. I have certainly spoken things to other people that should have stayed in Vegas, so to speak. So who am I to judge?

I wouldn't dare. You have not asked me to, but I forgive you. I will choose, over time, to rebuild our trust. I will believe the best, and, on the chance that you exhibit human frailties again, I will forgive you again. Fear has no place in friendship. I choose not to be afraid to risk relationship with another human being, so you don't need to be afraid of occasionally acting like one.

With love,

Lisa

Unfortunately, months later I learned that Lauren told my secrets to another mutual friend, even after my e-mail to her. I haven't cut off the friendship—there is so much worth saving—but I will never open my heart or life to Lauren again. It isn't safe. We have a fun friendship on the surface, but I am ever-cautious, and our bond is not the intimate one it once was of complete confidence and sharing.

The Telltale Signs

Since then, I have learned a few things about how to identify safe people. The telltale signs were there if I had only known what to look for. Of course, my first clue with Lauren should have been when she gossiped about other people to me.

I was incredibly naïve. If a man comes up to you

wearing a trench coat lined with gold watches on the inside, trying to sell them to you at a deal, you can't be shocked if you ask him to come over to your house for dinner and then discover the jewelry in your bathroom drawer is missing after he's left.

Now I know to pay attention to warning signs to discern unsafe areas. For instance, I listen closely to conversations with my friends. If they are loose-lipped, judgmental, petty, negative, or condescending while talking about someone else, then odds are they probably talk about me the same way when I'm not around.

By the same token, if someone looks for the best in people, gives them the benefit of the doubt, or doesn't join in when others gossip or gang up on a person who is not present, then I can know that person is probably safe holding my reputation even when I'm not there to protect it myself. Mary Graham says that "Ney Bailey is so confidential that she won't even tell me stuff I told her."

After having learned a few more things through the school of hard knocks, I realize there were also some warning signs I could have paid attention to in some of my earlier friendships. George, my Bible study teacher, explained that my emotional account was overdrawn. On a dry erase board, he drew a picture of a bank account. Then he showed me all of the people in my life who were withdrawing energy, emotions, thoughts, and time from that account—all the places where I was spending myself. Then he asked me where the deposits were coming in from to refill my reserves. This visual helped me see that, in most of the relationships in my life, I was giving out but not receiving enough to avoid emotional bankruptcy. It was critical that I get in relationship with some people who weren't only interested in receiving but who were also able to give and replenish me.

Ney calls this the Bucket-Thimble model. Some people have the capacity to contain a bucketful, some a cupful, and others a thimbleful. If I am able to hold a bucketful of resources and I am in a relationship with someone who is only capable of containing a thimbleful, then when I pour out of my ability, the thimble feels full to overflowing. Unfortunately, even if a thimble gives all that she is able to give, she just isn't capable of giving me all I need. That is not an indictment against her; there are surely understandable reasons for her relative or seasonal capacity. But I need to take an honest look and not expect more from her than she is able to give. I need to find another bucket, a few cups, or a handful of thimbles.

Another helpful hint I've learned is to pay attention to what somebody does, not just what she says. I know that sounds elementary, but this has been a hard thing for me to accept. I tend to want to believe someone's words to me, even when the actions don't align.

For instance, only recently was I able to let a friend *not* be my friend if she didn't really want that. Sound confusing? Stay with me on this. Let me tell you about a woman named

Karla whom I met on one of my speaking engagements. Karla was born and raised in Texas but had since moved to another state to help her husband pastor a church.

Immediately, Karla and I had clicked. We had each read the same books and loved to have philosophical discussions that had no beginning or end and were full of questions with very few answers. Besides that, Karla was just a whole lot of fun. We couldn't wait for the next opportunity for our paths to cross again. She promised to call the next time she came to town.

Now I knew she'd be coming home to spend the holidays with her folks in Fort Worth, so I assumed I'd hear from her so we could set up a time to meet for lunch or dinner while she was here. But the holidays came and went, and she never called.

Our paths crossed again a few months later, and we had another thoroughly enjoyable time together. Karla mentioned that she would be coming home for her niece's high school graduation and that we had to get together. So I sent her an e-mail at the first of May, asking if she thought she and her husband might have time to come over to our house for dinner. If not, I'd understand if all she could do was meet me for a quick cup of coffee.

No response.

Graduation came and went, and I knew Karla had come to town, but apparently she didn't have time to squeeze me into her schedule.

Believe me, I know how crazy family trips can get, and I know Karla probably was trying to be nice and not hurt my feelings. But I wish she had been a little bit more up-front with me. It would have been better for both of us if she could have said, "I really love talking to you when our paths cross, but my life is super busy and my friend basket is already crowded. I don't think I'll be able to get together with you when I come to town."

As it was, she did say those things . . . just not with her words.

Thankfully, I eventually learned to listen to actions as well as words and weigh them together more carefully.

Karla appeared to be a perfect Christian. That should have been my first unsafe person alert. I've since learned to look for people who can be real and honest about their shortcomings and struggles. There is no such thing as a perfect person, so if you think you are meeting one, run! Perfect people cannot connect with you at a real level because they cannot connect to themselves at a real level. That's why they must wear the mask of perfection.

If it is so important to them to give the illusion of per-fection then they will expect perfection from you too. That is not possible, and you will always feel "less-than" around them. One of the biggest lessons I've learned about safe friends is to pay attention to whether they are too hard on themselves or if they are judgmental toward other people. Usually, these two traits go hand-in-hand.

Grace Makes Connection Safe

I can't dare risk exposing my humanity with someone if she can't accept my imperfection. I recently had a friend tell me that someone she knew was selfish and lazy for not simply getting out of a sinful situation. "Why doesn't she just do the right thing?" my friend railed. "She obviously isn't trying hard enough. I wonder if she is even a Christian."

Note to self: *Don't confess your struggles with this friend—she's not safe.*

Two of my safest friends are Nancy McKeon and my hairstylist of more than twenty-five years, Michele Mason. Michele is safe precisely because she has blown it with the Lord big time and understands what it is to need the gift of grace. She also knows how to give and receive grace.

What makes Nancy safe is that even though she doesn't believe the same way I do, she respects my beliefs and loves that part of me though she has chosen a different path. Because of this, she knows how to give a friend room to be herself, not the person Nancy thinks she should be. Nancy allows ample space to make mistakes and mess up without freaking out. We don't go to the same church, but she takes God at his Word when he says that the greatest commandment is to love God and then love your neighbor as yourself. She does that better than almost anyone I know.

Another trait I look for in a safe friend is someone

who doesn't try to fix me. She knows that is God's job, not hers. A safe friend may question and challenge me. Remember the proverb "As iron sharpens iron, so one man sharpens another" (Proverbs 27:17)? This proverb reminds me that a solid, sharp person can solidify and sharpen me but not by tearing me down. A safe friend will live her life before you and trust God to move on your heart in his time and in his way. Certainly we are more influenced by who a person is than by what he or she says; sometimes God chooses to use us to speak through, but mostly he likes to live through us.

So just as a safe friend is not the one who tries to fix you, it's worth remembering that you cannot be a safe friend by trying to fix others either.

I had a friend, Katie, whom I adored, who really struggled in the area of taking responsibility. By nature, I like to jump in and make things happen, so I came alongside to help carry her load. After months of helping, I realized Katie wasn't one bit stronger. I had done all the heavy lifting. Ultimately, I had enabled her to remain weak and afraid. I had to step away until she at least took a few baby steps toward independence.

Don't get me wrong, I'm all for coming alongside someone who is struggling. When someone is in a hospital bed, I'm not going to say, "Get up and get your own blanket . . . and while you're at it, change that bandage and redress your wound." That would be cruel.

We need safe people we can lean on and be dependent upon during times of deep emotional suffering. There is a difference in feeling the need to rescue someone and being there for someone who is in the process of being rescued.

Unfortunately, the more broken we are, the more we need safe people in our lives, and yet that very brokenness often makes us more vulnerable to unsafe people. To make matters worse, brokenness left to itself makes us unsafe people to others. It's a terrible Catch-22. But, there is an answer.

Becoming a Safe Person

Hurt people hurt people. Even more than wanting to find safe people, I want to be a safe person. Of course, it is hard to have one want without exercising the other. These wants work hand in hand: you inevitably seek out friends with the same level of brokenness. That is one of the reasons it is so important to deal with our own issues. We want to have safe friends and be safe friends.

In my life, my distorted thinking tells me that if I make a mistake I will not only get in bad trouble but I will also be cut off from my source of love and life. Therefore, I must be perfect in order to avoid disconnection. Until I deal with this lie, I will unconsciously seek out close friends who have unattainable standards, and I will try with all I have and am to be perfect in order to keep a connection that feels like my very life depends upon it.

Henry Cloud writes:

> Distorted thinking was learned in the context of relationship, and that is the only place where it can be unlearned. You need new relationship to undo the learning of the past; there your real self can be connected in grace and truth and thereby be transformed.[1]

For me, this is happening in many of my relationships but in none more than my friendship with Ney. At first, whenever I made a mistake, an unchristian remark sneaked out, or a negative emotion crept up and spilled over, I would brace myself for judgment and correction. I would then pull back emotionally from Ney in order to protect myself from the pain of rejection and disconnection. Time and time again, my display of humanity caused her to step in a little closer, talk a little gentler, smile a little sweeter, open her heart a little more, and reveal a little more of her own struggles.

Dealing with our past and learning new ways of relating are very important if we want to be safe friends to others. For instance, I struggle with all-or-nothing reactions. This is a learned behavior from my past when bonding was inconsistent. I needed a stable connection in order to live, but it wasn't always available. At that point, I learned not to need it in order to survive the pain of disconnection.

The way this might play out in my present relationships could make me an unsafe friend if I don't deal with the origin of these feelings. Otherwise, I might hurt someone by either cutting them off and acting like I don't need them at all, or needing them so much that I feel like I will die if we can't connect. Since I ultimately want to live vulnerably and openhandedly, I need to experience healthy separateness in a safe relationship so that it doesn't scare me to the degree that I sever or cling.

It is hard for me to take an honest look at how many times I've unintentionally caused other people pain because I hadn't dealt with my own. I am learning how important it is to deal with our own broken places so we don't inadvertently break other people's hearts. This is necessary if we want to touch other people's hearts with God's love and healing. It is difficult to really touch someone if we are wearing a coat of armor to protect our wounds rather than exposing them and finding healing for them. Then we feel the need to dress up our layers of protection to disguise the fact that they are really just ugly shields.

The other day, I got to thinking about this. I've always operated under the mistaken notion that the more perfect I was, the more that people would like me and want to connect with me. So I kept a slick, glossy finish on my layer of protection. What I learned was, ultimately, my very shininess acted like Teflon and prevented any kind of lasting bond.

On the other hand, there is very little that holds more tightly than Velcro, which is full of loops, holes, and fuzz-catching texture. Not particularly attractive, Velcro will certainly stick, just like a true friend. You see, when I drop my shiny shield and let my holes, loopiness, and messy layers show, people get close to me and I am able to form solid attachments.

Much of what I have thought to be true all my life is turning out to be the exact opposite. My thinking has been distorted, and I didn't even realize it. I imagine it must be like a child feels who thinks a marking on the chalkboard is the number three, only to finally get prescription glasses and realize that the *3* isn't even a number at all but the letter *B*.

The safer we become, the safer we can help others become. In another Catch-22, we can't give grace unless we have received grace. Notice I didn't say unless we have been given grace. There is a difference in being given something and receiving it. With my track record of preferring to be on the giving end of the equation, coupled with my paranoia over making any mistakes, grace has been a tough gift to accept.

I remember when it became clear to me that God was trying to take me to a whole 'nother level of understanding grace. I actually said aloud, "God, I do want to receive grace. I just don't want to need grace . . . because that would mean that I messed up, and I so don't want to mess up."

Guess what. I messed up. But I received the message—and grace.

Nine

Afraid to Be Free

I've been a Christian for more than thirty-five years, but I wasn't able to comprehend God's radical grace until I opened my life up to friend-ships with safe people.

Before, I preferred the Law, playing at life by rules, measuring my worth by how godly a life I could live, try-ing to earn God's love. Rules always felt safer. There was right and wrong, black and white, lines to stay behind and never to cross. The Law was something I could hold on to that made me feel like I had some control in the midst of tumultuous emotions and circumstances. Yet deep down I wanted someone bigger and stronger to hold on to me during the frightening times of living in this world.

What God ultimately gave me was better than something safe to hold on to and even better than someone safe to hold on to me. He rooted me and grounded me in his love. He strengthened me in my inner being. He anchored my heart, as Ephesians 3:16-21 explains, to his in an exceedingly abundant relationship of grace.

As with all growth, coming to terms with Law versus grace in my faith has been a process. When my children were babies, I carried them everywhere in my arms. They had no freedom, no autonomy. When they learned to walk, I put a gate in front of the stairs and between the doorposts. They had freedom, but it was in a confined space. When they were toddlers, whenever I took them someplace where they could get lost, like the airport or the mall, I put little harnesses around their chests and kept them safe by holding on to the cord of their harnesses. They could run around freely but only as far as I felt was safe. Later, I held their hands.

Eventually, my children simply walked beside me . . . but still close enough that I could grab their hands if I felt they were in danger, such as when we walked through a parking lot. As they got older, I allowed them to play as long as I could keep an eye on them. Sometimes they played in the neighborhood but always within earshot so I could call them home.

These days my children are grown and independent. They go and come as they wish. I have no control over them. That is terrifying to me on one level, and on another level it is more deeply satisfying than I can explain. When they are with me, it is because they want to be with me. They need me or simply want me. Each stage of growth is good and necessary, but maturity is marked by more freedom, not less.

So it is for us as children of God: we are to grow closer to grace, not deeper bound to Law. The Law is important, foundational even (John 1:17). We can't just skip Law and go straight to grace. Then we wouldn't appreciate the gift or the cost to the Giver of the gift. The Law is the beautiful box in which the gift came wrapped. But we are to let God out of the box, out of our containing ideas of him, to know him personally in all his majesty and mystery. Only babies prefer playing with the box and paper a gift comes wrapped in. With understanding, there is enjoyment of the gift.

Paul talks about this in chapter four of Galatians, only he also uses the illustration that the Law is like a tutor when we are children (KJV). It tells us what to do and what not to do. It keeps us safe from harm. But when we grow up and act like dearly beloved children of God, we follow him from our hearts because we love him, or even more truthfully, because he first loved us. And we know it. We are safe because we are close to our Father—he is within us. This is the difference between living from the inside out of love and living from the outside out of fear.

Paul says in 1 Corinthians 13:11, "When I was a child, I talked like a child, I thought like a child, I reasoned like a child. When I became a man, I put childish ways behind me."

I am learning that the Bible actually says that we are to let go of the Law and embrace grace, or better yet, be embraced by grace. Of course, my first thought upon realizing what this meant was, "Yeah, but if I believe that, then what is going to keep me from sinning?"

Maybe "not sinning" isn't the primary goal. Maybe staying close to the Father is the goal—and the answer to that very question.

You see, it's all upside down. I thought that if I didn't sin then I would stay close to my Father. It is the other way around! If I stay close to the Father, I'm less likely to sin. If you really want to be confused, then join me as I ponder the truth that if I'm really, really close to the Father, as in "Christ is in me," then he sees me as if I haven't ever sinned and never will. Talk about risky freedom and dangerous grace!

I liked the Law. It felt less risky than grace. Grace felt too good to be true. I was afraid to trust it. I felt comfortable with the Law. Just tell me what to do so I can do it right and earn love and acceptance. Grace felt all backwards to me. Tell me what to do so I can do it wrong and realize I can't earn love but I can accept it.

Don't get me wrong, the Law does work. At the beginning of this friendship and faith journey, I wrote to a friend:

I feel like I am having a Damascus Road experience. This feels more like being born again than when, as a little girl, I took that first leap of faith and first trusted Christ as my Savior. I feel like all the right and good things I have done in my life have been blessed because God's ways work. Obedience works! But it is nothing compared to the blessing of knowing Jesus through his suffering and grace!

Being Held by Grace

Still, I'm afraid if I let go of the Law that I might fall. Transitioning from Law to grace is terrifying. There is that point in the middle when you wonder if grace is really true, and, if not, that could mean certain death. The illustration that helped me dare to let go of the safety of Law and to hope that I had grasped the correct concept of grace was when I read a conversation that author Henri Nouwen had with a famous flying trapeze artist:

One day, I was sitting with Rodleigh, the leader of the troupe, in his caravan, talking about flying. He said, "As a flyer, I must have complete trust in my catcher. The public might think that I am the great star of the trapeze, but the real star is Joe, my catcher. He has to be there for me with split-second precision and grab me out of the air as I come to him in the long jump." "How does it work?" I asked. "The secret," Rodleigh said, "is that the flyer does nothing and the catcher does everything. When I fly to Joe, I have simply to stretch out my arms and hands and wait for him to catch me and pull me safely over the apron behind the catchbar."

"You do nothing!" I said, surprised. "Nothing," Rodleigh repeated. "The worst thing the flyer can do is to try to catch the catcher. I am not supposed to catch Joe. It's Joe's task to catch me. If I grabbed Joe's wrists, I might break them, or he might break mine, and that would be the end for both of us. A flyer must fly, and a catcher must catch, and the flyer must trust, with out-stretched arms, that his catcher will be there for him."[1]

Grace requires such radical trust, and trust is almost impossible if most of your experiences have been of others letting you go or letting you down.

Yesterday, I was reading a book and underlined this statement: "The many loving Christians I have met in my life have had at least one unconditionally loving parent or friend along the way, and God was then able to second the motion."[2]

Once again, it comes back to the truth that growth and healing happen with the context of relationship. We are the body of Christ, and we will most often experience his love through the hands and heart of his body. It is easier to receive his grace and love and acceptance when we have some point of reference for what we're looking for or what it feels like. We need to see it in the face of another. It is as one of Ney's favorite quotations says: "Grace is nothing more nor less than the face that love wears when it meets imperfection, weakness, failure, sin."[3]

One morning, my younger daughter, Clancy, came downstairs and sat on the couch beside me. I could tell she was upset even before she said, "Mama, you taught me that if we bring sin into the light, that it takes away its power. I can't keep this inside me anymore. I need to get it out." Clancy proceeded to confess her struggle and failure in an area.

Although she was sixteen years old at the time, I scooped her up, put her in my lap, and held on tightly. I kissed the top of her head and thanked her for trusting me enough to invite me into her hidden places. I assured her that her imperfection only made me love her more.

She looked at me with tears in her eyes and said, "I think some mothers think they give birth to angels, and then when they mess up they think they are more like fallen angels. I'm glad that you know you gave birth to a human."

That touched my heart deeply. Isn't that what we all want? To be seen, in all our glory, for better or for worse; for the good, the bad, and the ugly—and to still be embraced and kissed and held?

I was reading the following passage just today:

What I let God see and accept in me also becomes what I can then see and accept in myself. And even more, it becomes that whereby I see everything else. This is 'radical grace.' This is why it is crucial to allow God, and at least one other person, to see us in our imperfection and even our nakedness, as we are— rather than as we would ideally wish to be. It is also why we must give others this same experience of being looked upon in *their* imperfection; otherwise, they will never know the essential and utterly transformative mystery of grace.[4]

The word *nakedness* is perfect to describe how it feels to bare your soul, even to a safe, grace-filled friend. I prefer to get undressed in the dark because I don't want anyone to see my stretch marks, varicose veins, and cottage cheese thighs; I go to great lengths to keep my unsightly bulges covered up, preferably in black or navy. So the thought of being naked, even emotionally, makes me want to run for the covers. Yet, as something I recently read says so beautifully, this is the quickest route to knowing grace in our innermost being:

If people know they are loved, they are not afraid of their "badness." They feel accepted and safe, and they do not have to feel "good" about themselves to be safe. Love does that. Love is everything. In the Bible, the opposite of "bad" is not "good." It is love.[5]

Allrighty then, let's get naked!

Ten

Let's Get Real

W hen we feel like we must be perfect to live up to the law then it is very tempting to wear a mask and put on a show. When I first learned that the word *hypocrite* originally meant *an actor*, I was only a tiny bit surprised and offended. In ancient Greece, a hypocrite was someone who wore a mask and played a part in a show.

Yep, sounds like a hypocrite to me.

I never thought of myself as a hypocrite until recently. As a matter of fact, I thought I was the opposite. I was trying very hard to practice what I preach. The irony was, in order not to be thought of as a hypocrite, I often pretended to be someone I wasn't—someone who didn't have problems and struggles, stinky attitudes, and sinful inclinations.

It wasn't until more recently, as I have begun learning about grace in friendships and transferring that experience to the Lord that I found the freedom to be not so perfect, to take off the mask. Again, I have only really learned how to let this truth make its way down from my head to my heart, through friendship.

My older daughter, Haven, sent this quotation to me last week. Her best friend sent it to her, and she knew I'd love it:

> True friendship is a sacred, important thing, and it happens when we drop down into that deeper level of who we are, when we cross over into the broken . . . fragile parts of ourselves. We have to give something up in order to get friendship like that. We have to give up our need to be perceived as perfect. We have to give up our ability to control what other people think of us. We have to overcome the fear that when they see the depths of who we are, they'll leave. But what we give up is nothing in comparison to what this kind of friendship gives to us. Friendship is about risk. Love is about risk. If we can control it and manage it and manufacture it, then it's something else. But if it's really love, really friendship, it is a little scary around the edges.[1]

Would you rather have a friend who is imperfect but real, or would you rather be in relationship with a perfect robot? Most of us want to live authentically, but the reality is more daunting than the proposition. It takes practice, trial and error, making mistakes and learning from them. Once again, this is where we need to have safe people in our lives. A place where we can be honest and truthful. The truth is what is real; it describes things as they really are. Not how we think they should be or how we think we should feel as good Christians.

We want friends whom we can call and say, "This is how I'm really feeling, this is the way it really is, this is who I really am." We want those friends who will accept us, just like that: all that we are, the good, the bad, the little bit of both. Each of us craves that.

What is interesting is that when we are really gut-honest with people about our frailties and failures, it makes them feel better about themselves. You know what I'm talking about. Have you ever gone over to a friend's house and her dirty dishes are in the sink and across the counter, her kids are fighting, and there is a sticky film of syrup still on the kitchen table? Doesn't it make you feel all warm and fuzzy about yourself inside?

What a gift that is! Give a present to your friends. Go without makeup. Wear your comfy jeans to lunch. Invite them over and leave your unfolded laundry on the couch. Trust them with your real self. Maybe they will risk doing the same with you. Pretty soon you will feel about each other the way you feel about an old pair of shoes. Easy. Comfortable. Your favorites.

One of the sweetest gestures a friend ever made toward me was when she vulnerably confessed an insecurity she felt about a friend in her life who hadn't responded to her last few e-mails. She contacted her friend with a very honest e-mail and then asked me to pray for her because she was nervous about how it would be received. When all was said and done, I sent her this note.

Hey sweet friend,

Can I tell you how much I appreciate being invited into the behind-the-scenes, under-the-surface, into-the-heart, from-the-inside-out perspective of this girlfriend drama e-mail exchange? I like being your friend. It is a privilege. You are special, and I feel special that I get to be your friend. I like knowing you— "know" as in intimate friendship. I feel unashamed when you see my immature, naked, insecure emotions, and then I feel closer to you. But, today I thank you for letting me "know" you, as in being known. By revealing your honest trepidation as you sent the e-mail, your courage as you steeled yourself for possible disappointment, and then your joy of knowing all was well, you were a friend. You could have taken this short journey by yourself, but instead you invited me to join you. We may not live close enough to say, "Hey, jump in the car with me. I'll buy you a mocha if you'll keep me company while I run errands." But, we can say, "Hey, read this quick e-mail and walk alongside me while we do life together, six hundred miles apart."

Love you,

Me

When people think we are perfect, without insecurities or faults, it works against connection. Vulnerability creates connection faster than almost anything. I don't remember where I read it, but I love the definition that says "intimacy=into-me-see."

That makes me think of 2 Corinthians 6:11, where Paul says, *"We have spoken freely to you, Corinthians, our heart is wide open"* (ESV).

Four Friendship Necessities

While the first necessary quality for authentic friendship is opening up the heart and inviting in another person to look around and see the real you, the second quality is being accepted and understood.

Being understood is one of our deepest needs. We don't really need to know that we are "right" as much as we need to know that someone understands how we feel and what our "reality" is. Making this connection with each other is called "empathy." When we feel a certain way, we need to know that others validate our experience, meaning that they understand how it is for us.[2]

A few nights ago, I received a phone call from a friend I grew up with. She asked if we could just drive around and talk. As soon as I hopped in her car, she broke down, "Lisa, I feel like I'm in a prison. I don't know if I love my husband anymore. I'm screaming at my children all day. I want out, but I don't want to leave."

We pulled over to the side of the road, and I spent the next few minutes sharing with her times when I have felt the same way. I told her stories of when my kids were smaller, my husband was busy at work, and I felt isolated and alone, like the worst wife and mother in the world. I didn't give her any advice or Scripture verses. I simply gave her empathy and understanding. Mostly, I listened.

A few days later I called just to check in to see how she was doing. Her circumstances hadn't changed, but she was feeling better. Just getting it off her chest and sharing her burden with someone else made her feel lighter and able to journey on.

I think that is one of the things that makes Alcoholics Anonymous successful. They simply share where they are and receive each other as they are. Then they say, "Thank you," and "Next." There is healing power in being heard.

The third essential quality for authentic friendship is

the gift of having someone who will be honest with you about you. A few months ago, Jennifer suggested that whenever we get to be together in the same town, we could continually strengthen our friendship by taking the opportunity to ask each other three specific questions.

She began, "One. What do you see in my life that encourages you?"

I responded: "I see you being willing to ask the hard questions of yourself and of life and, ultimately, of God. You don't want to live in a Pollyanna world of denial. You want the truth, the whole truth, and nothing but the truth, so help you, God."

"Okay, two," she ventured. "What do you see in my life that you would caution me about?"

I had to think a long time about this one, but then, in gentle honesty, I said: "When you write in your journal, be as raw and unfiltered as possible. You may eventually end up using your thoughts and reflections in a future book, but don't journal with an end result in mind."

"Good, thanks," she said. "Three, What else would you like to say?"

"Without hesitation," I said, "that I love getting to be your friend on your journey!"

Since this first conversation, we have asked each other these questions a few more times, and—without fail—they have drawn us closer.

Psychologists Henry Cloud and John Townsend

know this is a recipe for healthy friendships. On their Web site, they recommend you ask a couple of questions periodically in your relationships: What do I do that draws me to you? What do I do that pushes you away?[3]

Reading this, I picked up the phone and called my friend Marilyn Meberg to ask her these two risky but rich questions.

"Oh, I don't like that first question!" she responded in her inimitable way. "It isn't what you do that draws you to me. It is who you are. I feel a commonality with you. We are kindred souls, even though you are almost thirty, fifty, or eighty years younger than me. You love to process. You love to ask the *why* questions, more than the *what* questions. There is reciprocity. You get me. Now, what do you do that pushes me away? Maybe I could sometimes interpret your actions as not being interested in pursuing a friendship—unless you initiate times for us to get together."

This was very helpful to me because I hadn't realized that my being so busy writing this book lately and not reaching out to make contact with my friends could be misinterpreted as disinterest. I'm so glad I asked this question. We immediately made a lunch date for the Friday after my book deadline!

This brings us to the final essential ingredient for authentic friendships: having a friend who will be honest about what she is feeling in herself and in the relationship, even if that means it might get a bit sticky for a minute or two. Ultimately, we don't want a friend who always says yes or only what she thinks we want to hear. I want a friend who will tell me where she wants to eat or what she wants to do or not do.

If I love someone, I want to know how she feels and what she needs. It feels much safer to me to have a friend who will speak up and tell me when she is frustrated with me or when I've hurt her feelings than to have one who pretends that everything is okay in the name of being "nice."

Not that we have to share every fleeting feeling that passes through our hormones. It was a humongous discovery for me when I learned that I don't have to react to all of my emotions. I went on a Silent Retreat last year, and in the quiet, the Holy Spirit revealed a truth to me that set me free. This is what I recorded in my journal:

Another big lesson I've learned on this retreat is that I can allow feelings to surface, feel them deeply and completely, but I don't need to "do" anything with them! If anger were to rise up, it wouldn't have to overwhelm me. I could let it come up, feel it, and let it keep going through me and out of me. I don't need to fear hurting anyone with my anger because I have the choice not to react in anger or say what I'm feeling, unless I decide to.

When hurt surfaces, I don't have to run away or

withdraw or devise a plan not to feel hurt again. I can feel it, grieve it, let it go, and know that the feeling will eventually go away. There is an end. I don't have to stuff it or deny it or express it or obey it.

But, when I do need to vent, I want a friend who can handle my honesty. I want to be the safe person friends come to when they are afraid to be real with anyone else. Remember, your honesty is a gift, and it encourages others to be authentic with you. I received the following e-mail from Jennifer when I first approached her about going to the next level of disclosure with each other.

Dear Lisa,

Here's what I have pondered since our talk this a.m.: Do I have anyone in whom I honestly confide? No, I don't tell anyone my deepest struggle with sin. No one ever asked. I don't think I ever realized that before today. I confess to no one but Jesus. I am not certain that is biblical.

I feel a little discomfort even as I admit how little I admit! So, I guess that's why the last part of our conversation struck me so. No one has ever asked me to engage in a truly honest, accountable relationship. Isn't that interesting? I never noticed that was the case until I really thought about it. I guess that standard has been presumed but never laid out that frankly. That's why I've been able to keep a degree of guarded honesty with others—it was assumed that I was giving the whole deal. Hmm.

So, I am taking seriously your suggestion to be honest and accountable. I respect you and trust you and I can go there with you. I take words and people very seriously, so I will do my best with this.

Now I think I need a Starbucks!

So, may I invite you to take the plunge into authentic friendship? Before you jump, let me caution you about one thing. Shallow waters are easier to swim in than deeper depths. Allow me in the next chapter to share a few techniques I've learned for keeping friendships afloat during times of stormy conflict that can be stirred up by honest conversations.

Eleven

Conflict Can Be a Good Thing

I hate conflict. My whole life I've avoided it. This has actually proven pretty successful. I am well-liked. Life is relatively peaceful. My friendships are fun and easy. One minor problem: I'm not quite sure where I lost Lisa along the way.

As you already have surmised, I have tended toward extremes in my life. In the past, I have either had strong, nearly impenetrable boundaries by cutting off need, hiding behind a book, or running off to my dressing room. Or, I've swung too far the other way, trying to stay connected by attempting to please everyone but losing myself in the process.

Not everyone in your life will want honest friendship with you, especially friends who are used to getting what they want in the relationship. They probably won't like it if you change the dance and start speaking up about things. I have lost a few friends who couldn't flex with the new me. This still hurts. I want everyone to like me, and I don't want anybody to be mad at me. I just don't want to have to be somebody else for that to be possible. I want to be authentic. I want to be loved and accepted for who I am. To do that, I need to know who I am and be brave enough to be different from you.

I have discovered this is easier said than done. So, I am taking baby steps. Even saying what I want is a boundary. It separates me from you; it defines me. A boundary is also not a punishment. That truth has helped me a lot. Rather, a boundary is a protection. I can simply say, "If you continue to _____ (fill in the blank), then in order to take care of myself, I will have to _____ (fill in the blank)." This is not a consequence—that could border on manipulation. No, this kind of healthy boundary-setting is self-care. It answers the question we would all be wise to ask in unwanted situations: What will I do to take care of myself?

Of course, this smacks right up against what I've been taught all my life: I am to prefer others above myself. God has used a handful of instances to help me find that both of these teachings can coexist. One time, I felt the need to express my opinion within the context of authentic friendship, even though I knew well and good that my friend wouldn't approve and would be mad at me. And she was.

Later, she came to me and shared how God had used me to help her experience a deep healing in an area she had been able to avoid. In this, and many situations, by being true to who I am, God has ultimately used me in someone's life to bless her at a much deeper level than if I had laid down my life for her.

A Brick at a Time

One of the many things my friend Ney has taught me is to love conflict. Okay, well, I won't go that far. I still don't love conflict, but Ney's taught me not to hate it and to see how conflict can be a good thing, an opportunity for closer connection. Thankfully, she is a wise, patient teacher, and in this arena there is a learning curve.

In Ney's book *Faith Is Not a Feeling*, she writes about taking care of issues that arise in relationships by dealing with them "a brick at a time."[1] As Ney explains it, bricks represent a disagreement here, a misunderstanding there, differences that naturally occur in any relationship between two unique people. But once the brick has been discovered, you must deal with it. Now it's easy to ignore an issue at first, thinking it's too small or petty and not worth making a big deal about it. But time and neglect or apathy or denial are exactly what enable one brick to remain, and then another, until there's a pile or the bricks are so heavily laid one upon the other that you can wake up to find a brick wall of separation built between you and another person.

Once a wall starts appearing, you either walk away from one another, because who can walk through walls. Or you have an explosive argument to blast though the brick wall—and at least one person, if not both of you, is going to be wounded by the blast, bruised in the rubble, or buried in the dust.

I love this "brick-at-a-time" concept so much that I have started to take care of all the bricks and become a little obsessive about picking up even grains of sand in my friendships or sweeping away the lightest dust. Not that we have to bring up every little thing. But I like how it feels to know that there is nothing between us that could interfere with safe, honest connection. It is always difficult to bring up issues that never seem to get any easier, but I know how good it feels afterwards, so it makes the hard work worth it.

Recently, I was having dinner with a dear, dear friend. I admire her terribly and hold her in the highest esteem for the interior and exterior lives she leads. We were reminiscing about the treasure of our friendship and what a gift it is to have friends who are safe, allowing each of us to be completely ourselves and at ease.

At this point during the conversation, I sensed a brick lying between us. Then I stopped myself: *A brick? Really? Surely, I'm imagining things . . .*

It would have been so easy to give in to my hesitation, to hold back a little of myself and give in to fear of daring to even raise a possible issue. After all, there was so much good in the friendship, and who am I to judge anyway?

Yet I knew that if I didn't say something, a wall of unspoken, negative feelings could rise between us. The only way to remove this wedge was to bring it out into the light and speak the truth in love.

So, I held my breath and said: "Oh, I do value the years of trust our friendship has built. I know you love me and there is nothing you wouldn't do for me, if you could. But if I am to be very honest with you, I don't know that I really do feel as completely safe with you as I would like. Maybe it is my problem, but I would be afraid to tell you some of my darker thoughts and secrets. My instinct tells me that you would feel the need to fix me by sharing Scripture with me to bring light to my dark places and help me walk the straight and narrow path more easily. The truth is, I know what the Bible says. There are times I just need a friend to love me and accept me the way I am, without trying to help me get all cleaned up first."

Oh my goodness, that was *so* hard to say. But I valued our friendship enough to take care of this brick before a wall had a chance to be built by things being left unsaid, feelings being left unaddressed, or issues being covered up in the name of being nice and not judging.

The next week my friend wrote this to me:

When I left you after dinner last week, I knew that a new Lisa has emerged—a softer version of the one I've known for twenty years. I could sense the absence of a wall around your heart: more vulnerable, gentler, kinder. Not that I ever perceived you as unkind or harsh, but there was a softness that was new. Even when you spoke into my life by telling me you felt you couldn't trust me because of my possible response of fixing it rather than empathizing with you, there was no doubt of your love and respect for me. Just the fact you were so honest was new and refreshing, a sign of your own new vulnerability in relationship to me. You took a risk that not many friends have the courage to do. Thank you for that.

I certainly never would have coupled the words *gentle* or *kind* or *soft* with conflict resolution. From my experience, it always had to be harsh or extreme or hurtful. Ironically, in almost every situation where I have taken the initiative to confront issues before they grew, the result has been a more tender, yet more solid, relationship. Another principle Ney writes about in her book and has since taught me is the concept of imagination balloons. For instance, the other day I called Ney, and she seemed very distracted, like she didn't want to talk to me. She asked if she could call me back later.

In my mind, I immediately imagined what she must be feeling and jumped to this train of thinking: *I'm annoying her. I'm calling her too much. She has so many good friends and I'm like the irritating little sister who insists on tagging along when the older sister would rather be left alone to hang with the big girls.*

When she called back, I felt myself withdraw to protect myself. Of course, the little girl in me went straight to thinking: *Fine. If she doesn't want to be my friend anymore, then I don't want to be hers.*

Ney sensed my retreat and asked if I was okay.

I insisted there was nothing wrong.

Later on in the conversation, I acted like a big girl and responded like she had taught me to when I experience these kinds of conversations in my head, when I fill in the other person's dialogue with what I imagine she is feeling or thinking.

I finally confessed and said, "Ney, when I called earlier, I felt like you didn't want to talk to me because I was annoying you and that you probably would rather be talking to Mary or Luci. Is there any truth to that analysis?"

I heard her smile through the phone. "I am so glad you asked me about this," she said. "Here's what happened: I was making eggs, bacon, and toast for dinner, and the minute that you called, the eggs were ready, the toast popped up, and I was turning the bacon. I needed to get everything off the stove before it overcooked, and then I wanted to eat it while it was hot. I just finished my delicious breakfast for dinner, and now I'm calling you. I'm very proud of you for not letting this imagination balloon go unpopped."

All that I had imagined really didn't have any basis in reality! It was like a balloon full of nothing. By daring to ask whether my perceptions were true or not, I was able to pop the balloon.

When we don't take care of these misses, they can create an imaginary airbag between us. We can't put our finger on what the problem is, but we can certainly feel the distance between us.

Work Things Out Together

Without ever saying it out loud, I think I always felt like the goal of dealing with a disagreement, rather than sweeping it under the rug, was to determine who was right and who was wrong and then for forgiveness to flow whichever direction was decided.

Once, Ney showed me an illustration to help me envision the goal of conflict resolution. She put a Pepsi can in the middle of the table between us, illustrating a disagreement or misunderstanding that has happened. It is the same can that we both see, but our points of view are different. Then she said, "Lisa, tell me how you see the situation and what happened and how you felt. Then I will take a turn and tell you my perception and how I feel."

She taught me that the goal must always be toward understanding each person's perspective and empathy for each other's feelings. Then you continue to talk and listen until you can reconnect and move forward together. This process isn't about drawing dividing lines. Rather, it's about, as 1 Peter 3:7 explains, learning how to dwell together in an understanding way.

Unfortunately, I had an opportunity to put this conflict resolution tool into practice shortly after learning it. I had just begun traveling with Women of Faith, and most of The Porch Pals and Back Porch gals were on Twitter. I had been following them and getting to know them for a few months through their Tweets, but I didn't know anyone personally very well yet.

It didn't take long for me to recognize that Sheila Walsh is absolutely hysterical. Her Tweets make me laugh right out loud in public places. One morning, she uncharacteristically Twittered three very serious Tweets in a row: a Bible verse, a prayer, and a beautiful quote.

In an effort to be quick and clever, I shot off a reply Tweet to Sheila: "Well, didn't someone wake up on the holy side of the bed this morning."

"Not holy," came Sheila's quick reply. "Just grateful."

Oops. I instantly realized by her terse response that I

had been too flippant in my Tweet. I could tell that my sarcasm had wounded her, and I felt awful.

Sheila, however, is gracious and forgiving. So I thought for a moment that I could ignore this and it would go away in time. But in reality, it might go south and not *away* at all. The quick exchange was a brick between us, and if Sheila and I were to have the best chance at a healthy friendship, I was going to need to risk revisiting the misunderstanding to understand both sides of the miss.

The next time we were face to face, I asked if we could talk about what happened. I started with my side of the Pepsi can, how I had only known her to have witty Tweets and I was trying to be funny, too, but failed miserably. I really wanted to set things right and for us to better understand each other.

She then shared her perspective. She had awakened to some difficult news that morning: a friend of hers was terminally ill. Almost immediately after she received the news, she got on Twitter to post the prayer and Bible verse. When she received my response she thought, "Why do I make myself vulnerable like this? It only opens you up to misunderstanding and hurt. I don't even want to be on Twitter anymore. It isn't worth it."

I was so grateful to hear her perspective. In the process, I learned so many lessons. For one: you have to earn the right to be playful. Sheila didn't yet know my heart, so all she could do was take my words at face value. Another lesson is in the very nature of social media, how it can be wonderful for connection but has the major drawback of not showing the faces and hearts behind the connection, like when your tongue is planted firmly in your cheek. (Of course, at the point I sent my Tweet, not even my tongue-in-cheek could have been seen behind the foot in my mouth!) While Twitter allowed Sheila to show her hilariously hysterical side, it failed to capture her extremely tender, deeply spiritual side.

Hearing one another's hearts over the matter allowed us to hug without stumbling over the start of a brick wall in the way. But dealing with this brick wasn't simple or without discomfort, even pain. If not for being terribly embarrassed and unable to eat for two days for feeling so bad about hurting Sheila, it would have been easy to gloss over this little miscommunication. The last thing I wanted to do was bring it into the open and talk about it, causing possibly more hurt, more pain. I just wanted the incident to disappear. She barely knew me and didn't feel comfortable enough bringing it up either. But Ney encouraged me to get a clearer picture of Sheila's heart and to allow her to see mine.

The result not only rid us of the brick between us but also began a solid connection with a friend based on truth and grace.

Twelve

From Head to Heart

*H*ave you ever been with a friend and you know she's not really there, not truly present? Instead, she's a million miles away, in thought, perhaps the past, maybe the future, but in any case elsewhere, her own little world. What disconnection, even if all the right words are coming out of your mouths.

I've been wondering lately if this isn't one of the many reasons God sent his Son to be *with* us. I've been thinking about what it means to be present, and I keep coming to the idea that it is a gift, a gift so important to God that he even named his little boy Immanuel, *God with Us*.

Jesus didn't stay in his own heavenly world. He stepped into ours to be fully present, all there, 100 percent *with* us. Is that not the truest definition of the friendship we have with him? Is that not the model?

I am learning that an easy place to exercise my presence-practicing muscles is within friendships. When I am with a friend, I want to be fully engaged with her. Eyes connected, ears attuned, opinions on hold, mouth in neutral, heart wide open. The more in-the-moment encounters I have on the human level, the easier it is for me to be *with* Immanuel, in an incarnational way. Not worrying about the future or regretting the past. Not trying to think the right thoughts or say words that will cause him to act. Just being with him.

I think Jesus really likes that. I know I do. It touches my heart when someone makes room in her busy life to be with me. I know what that costs. Our time is so valuable and every one of us is spread so thin in a million important ways. In today's economy, to give someone your time is worth much more than money can buy.

I'll never forget the time one of my dearest friends called me and could hear distress in my voice. I didn't need to experience what I was going through alone. Although she was in the middle of shopping at Target, she left her basket full of items, got in her car, and came straight to my house. I needed her with me, and she knew it.

True friends understand the difference between the times you say, "If you ever need anything, don't hesitate to ask," and the other times when it says more to just show up.

My friend Angela and I experienced this. When she

received some devastating news, she called to share it with me through tears of confusion. As foolhardy as it sounds, I used my airline miles and booked a flight departing first thing the next morning; then I called her and declared, "I am on my way to be with you through this, unless you tell me no. I arrive at 10:30."

That same year, at an especially low point for me on the journey, Angela couldn't hop on a plane, so she sent me the gift of being with me through the mail. She put together one large box containing many tiny, individually wrapped presents. One was a cookbook with her favorite handwritten recipes along with a note that said, "When you love someone, you cook for them. Until I can cook for you, enjoy my famous waffles." Another gift was an angel along with a card that said, "Friends are like angels. Thanks for being my angel on earth." I had so much fun opening each gift and knowing she was so *with* me. My favorite present was a cheap, rhinestone tiara with a noted Scripture verse: "To all who mourn in Israel, he will give a crown of beauty for ashes" (Isaiah 61:3 NLT).

Yes, there is such a thing as *withness*, and it can be sent FedEx.

Don't Be Afraid to Ask

Sometimes I know that I need a friend but just hate to ask. Especially when I don't even really know what I need. I just know that I can't find what I'm looking for all by myself, and I don't want to be alone. I want to be with someone.

Earlier this morning, while waiting in the Starbucks drive-through, I sent my friend Kimmie a text message: "Nothing urgent at all, but if you find yourself with a few minutes, and you're feeling up to it, could you give me a call when you get a chance?"

Within five minutes, my cell phone rang with her sweet voice on the other end. After making sure I wasn't interrupting anything important, I jumped in, "Kimmie, I don't even know how I'm feeling, but one thing I do know is whenever I'm having a hard time understanding myself, you help me just by listening with your heart and hearing mine. I don't really even want to say the words out loud that I'm thinking because I have a sneaking suspicion that they are very selfish and immature and not at all how Jesus would feel if he were in my situation."

I proceeded to unload every jumbled thought and entangled emotion that was strangling my soul on the inside. And, as usual, by the end of the conversation I felt a hundred pounds lighter. It really wasn't anything in particular that Kimmie said. She just has a gift of being with me in the middle of my messiness; she convinces me that she hears what I'm saying and understands how I'm feeling.

Even though she is three hundred miles away, you see, she is absolutely *with* me.

Still I do wish I could have shared my cup of Starbucks

with her across the table. There is no substitute for being with someone in person, especially when you feel your "aloneness" so acutely. We can't always be together with a friend in person or even over the phone, but we can always be together in spirit. This is especially obvious in the area of prayer.

Why is it that we sometimes hesitate to ask our friends to help us carry our burdens through prayer? I received an e-mail from a friend who apologized for bothering me, but she really needed prayer. She then listed three huge things that had happened to her or her family over the last six weeks.

Six weeks she had carried these burdens all alone, when her friends could have helped carry the load. Of course friends pray for one another. I reminded her not to wait so long next time. This is what friends are for, to bolster one another. Later, I wrote her a tongue-in-cheek e-mail to illustrate my point that I sure wish she had written me from the get-go when she first needed prayer rather than wait so long:

Dear friend,

I hope I'm not bothering you but could you pray for me? A small F5 tornado ran through our neighborhood last month and ripped the roof off of our house. Thankfully, we only lost the Christmas decorations we had stored in the attic, but it is a bit of a nuisance when it rains. Well, then, our family kitten had her wisdom teeth

167

pulled last week and, of course, they were impacted and then she got dry sockets so it has been a real CATastrophe. The final straw came today when I discovered that evil hackers hacked into my Web site and added twenty pounds to all of the pictures of me on my site! That's when I got your e-mail, and it crossed my mind that maybe I should ask my friends to pray with me.

Your friend,

Lisa

Let's put pride and fear aside, and dare to reach out and admit our need for each other. Trust me, a real friend considers it an honor to be there in a time of need. Praying with one another is one of the highest privileges of friendship. In turn, connection is one of the mightiest privileges of prayer. Jesus says, "If two of you agree on earth about anything they ask, it will be done for them by my Father in heaven. For where two or three are gathered in my name, there am I among them" (Matthew 18:19 ESV).

One of the things I've learned from Ney is that discernment is for the purpose of prayer. When a need comes to our attention, whether through something we notice in someone or a situation that is brought to our awareness, we try to stop right then and there and pray about it together. This helps curb the temptation to gossip or judge. It also ensures that we actually pray and not just say we will and then forget to do it. Or like I've done before, say "I prayed for you," but what I really mean is *I thought about praying for you and sincerely meant to do it and doesn't that count as almost the same thing?*

As I've mentioned, being *with* someone doesn't actually require that we are physically with the other person. It also doesn't require words. As a matter of fact, words can sometimes get in the way of just *being* together. A few months ago, I was sitting on The Porch at a Women of Faith conference. My friend and *American Idol* singer Mandisa was seated beside me. She glanced over and noticed the tears welling up in my eyes even though I was fighting to keep them from falling onto my cheeks.

Intuitively, she knew not to say anything or ask me any questions. I would have become a blubbering idiot (which definitely would have been a distraction from the person on the platform). Instead, she scooted her chair over closer to mine, opened up the Snuggie that she wears because it is usually so cold in the arenas, and gave me one of the sleeves. She then proceeded to lay her head on my shoulder, and I laid mine on top of hers. Nothing was ever said, but she comforted my heart by being with me.

In that moment, she was my St. Francis of Assisi, who said, "Preach the gospel always. If necessary, use words." And then, Henri Nouwen writes:

When we honestly ask ourselves which persons in our lives mean the most to us, we often find that it is those who, instead of giving much advice, solutions, or cures, have chosen rather to share our pain and touch our wounds with a gentle and tender hand. The friend who can be silent with us in an hour of despair or confusion, who can stay with us in an hour of grief and bereavement, who can tolerate not-knowing, not-curing, not-healing and face with us the reality of our powerlessness, that is a friend who cares.[1]

These are the kinds of friends I have so desperately needed and still need. I am in the muddy mire and mystery of process. How grateful I am for friends who are willing to be with me in the middle of the mess before I'm all cleaned up.

Resting in Love

When I met Ney, I felt like such a mess. I had no way of earning her love, and she didn't seem to need mine. She wasn't impressed that I had been on a television show; she was a missionary in Eastern Europe during the eighties. I didn't need to perform in any way to earn her love, even though all my life—as an actress and Christian, family member, and friend—I'd worked and tried really hard to be deserving of love and acceptance. I didn't feel like I could give Ney anything, but she still chose to be my friend. She just liked me for me.

Every once in a while, she will stop in the middle of a

conversation, smile affectionately, and say, "Lisa, you delight my heart in a million ways."

This never fails to touch me at my core. In the beginning, I would think to myself, *Okay, now what did I just do so I can be sure and do it again so she will keep liking me?* But, she was never consistent with when she would say it. It was so random. As if it didn't have anything to do with anything I did or didn't do. So eventually the truth sunk in: she likes me, just me, for me. She chooses to be with me because she wants to, not because I deserve it, even when I mess up, even when I'm far from perfect.

One morning I was reflecting on this and said aloud: "God, when Ney tells me that I delight her heart in a million ways, her words heal me in deep places. That sounds like you. What doesn't sound like you is *when* she says it— when I'm acting foolish or childish or naughty. I can't imagine, God, that you delight in those things."

Immediately a picture came to my mind. I'm not talking about a vision. I mean a real photograph picture. I thought of a snapshot I took of my two little girls when they were ages four and five. I had set them up in the backyard with a double-sided easel and some paints while I worked in the kitchen. At one point, I looked out the window and could no longer see them. I went out the back door to discover them behind our storage shed. They had entirely stripped down and were completely naked, taking turns painting each other's bodies from head to toe. Being the avid scrapbooker that I am, I snuck inside to get my camera so I could take a picture of their body art. It was an adorable photo, a snapshot that I had enlarged last Christmas and placed in a frame with an engraving at the base that reads, "Well-behaved Women Rarely Make History."

Never mind that my girls are both grown and nearly out of the house. I love that picture. So when God brought it to my mind, I understood what he was saying to me. When my little girls were acting foolish, childish, and a wee bit naughty, they still delighted my heart because they were my daughters and I didn't expect them to be perfect.

In the same way, Ney's love for me when I exhibit those same traits is a natural demonstration of God's supernatural love. God delights in us—we don't have to be perfect.

Last week I was riding to dinner with Ney. She was telling me of a heartbreaking e-mail she had received about a young child. Something deep within me identified with the child in the story and made me bury my face in my hands. I knew that what I was feeling was shame. I couldn't pry my hands away from my face, and as she drove along in silence, I kept my face covered.

I thought: *I can't stay like this all night. We are almost to the restaurant. I'm going to have to find a way to lower my hands.*

I turned my face to look out the window and slowly removed my hands but couldn't turn my face back toward the center. I could feel Ney continually stealing glances from the road to look at me from the driver's seat, so I asked her, "Would you mind not looking at me while I look straight ahead?"

But I still couldn't face the road ahead. I couldn't turn my face from the shadows of the passenger door, so I closed my eyes, like a child does when she plays hide-and-seek and thinks that if she can't see anyone, then she cannot be seen either. Silently, I prayed: *Lord, I invite you into my shame. Rather than cover up my nakedness, I will step into your throne room. I need grace. I need mercy.*

Distinctly, tenderly, I heard him say: *Little one, you delight my heart in a million ways.*

In that instant, the feeling of shame was lifted, and I felt free to uncover my face. God was before me and behind me, above me, and below. He had my back and my future, was ready to pull me to higher living and catch me if I fell. He was present, and he was *with* me. And so was Ney, my Emmitt, right here alongside me.

I know, beyond a shadow, beyond a doubt, that friendship is a journey, as is faith. I would not have been able to hear or believe those words from the Lord before taking the steps toward being a friend and receiving one.

Henry Cloud expresses so beautifully and succinctly how to recognize God in the face of friendship:

We see this continually in clinical practice, especially among Christians who can't sense any closeness to

God . . . Only after they have worked on connecting to healthy people do they gradually begin sensing God more. They learn the spiritual truths only when the physical ones are in place.[2]

By experiencing Ney's love, grace, and acceptance in the middle of my shame and fears, I have been able to accept and embrace myself, my whole self, my broken self. Now I have a point of reference for receiving God's unconditional love and grace.

By God's enabling power, I pray that I will be able to represent his love and reflect his grace to others as they have done the same for me. I received the following e-mail recently from a friend. These words couldn't have been written except for the love of God that friends have poured into me that now overflows from my life:

Dear Lisa,

Because of your sharing with me your journey of beginning to grasp the amazing grace of God these past two years, and my seeing, hearing and feeling the fruit of it all over you, I've got to tell you, Lisa—you have rocked my world. When I began to say something that was obviously fleshly and unpleasing to the Lord, you shocked me by telling me how God delights in me. This was spoken by a friend who has experienced God's grace in a profound way herself. I'm still

processing that one (how that can possibly be true?),
but because of how God has revealed His grace and
mercy to you like never before, you have provoked me
to find more of it for myself.

Thank you.

It is my hope that in sharing with me my awkward
journey of these last few years you will embrace your own
neediness and shame and fears and insecurities and hopes
and longings for deeply connected friendships. I hope you
realize that your weakness is the perfect starting place for
growing in intimacy.

Know Thyself

May I encourage you to value intimacy with yourself as
much as intimacy with God and others? When you talk to
yourself, please be both honest and gentle. I needed help
to know myself. Consider inviting a trusted counselor,
guide, pastor, or mentor into your secret places, perhaps
even ones you've hidden from your own sight.

I would love to know that you are opening yourself up
to more vulnerability with old friends and taking the risk
to reach out and develop new friends. But first, please
make sure you've learned a thing or two about how to discern safe people in whom to entrust your heart. Listen

carefully and watch them without judgment but with wide-open eyes before you open wide your life.

I wish for you authentic relationships where you can dare to tell and hear the truth—where conflict is merely a precursor to your next step of growth and more intimate connection. And because you know this to be true, you can initiate difficult conversations in order to understand each other's perspective, to feel and then forgive, and to begin again at a deeper level.

My desire is that you will find friends who love to be with you and with whom you can connect, whether you're in the same room together or separated geographically. And, as only God could answer, I pray that you feel me with you on your journey and that you will come alongside me on mine.

As I mentioned at the beginning of this book, I am still in the middle of my journey. Maybe being on a journey means there is always more road ahead; maybe we are always moving toward a goal and discovering that what looks like the destination is simply another corner to turn. Rather than feeling disappointed, though, know that those corners and turns promise more adventure.

For me, this adventure in friendship has included many bumps in the road. Thankfully, it has also been marked by a few rough patches being made smooth. For instance, Heather and I have come to a comfortable place of mutual forgiveness and understanding. We have turned a corner, and I can see fresh possibilities for a new beginning while we still bring with us lessons from our past.

Obviously, I'm no longer on my writing sabbatical. I am carrying the stillness of being into the busyness of doing. I value my relationships over productivity these days. I believe with all my heart that although we may not be able to measure the invisible worth of investing time in people, there are few endeavors of more eternal significance.

I am finally grasping the love of Christ which passes understanding. It has worked its way down from a head knowledge to a heart experience that is transforming me. In fact, I barely recognize myself. Being good is no longer more important than being connected—with God, myself, and with others. I can be real, even real ugly and selfish and sinful, and then believe the truth that I am still loved and lovable.

This transition happened for me in the throne room of grace. Whenever I find myself in sin, either new or simply newly aware of, I force myself to imagine walking with confidence to "the throne of grace . . . so that we may receive mercy and find grace to help us our time of need" (Heb. 4:16). I don't cower in fear or shame. I choose to believe that nothing I could ever do could change the way God feels about me. He adores me. He delights in me. Even in the middle of my sin.

God feels the same way about you, his precious daughter.

Friends help us find our way there. I can't imagine walking into the throne room of grace if I had not been first welcomed into the hearts of grace of my friends. I know that faith is believing in what we can't see, but I'm grateful that God knows that we sometimes need a little glimpse in order to have a little faith.

Friends have been the visible manifestation to me of God's grace.

May God grant you an incarnation of his love through the gift of intimate friendships.

Questions for Reflection or Discussion

CHAPTER ONE: I NEED FRIENDS

1. In what ways do your grown-up friendships still feel like junior high?
2. Do you ever find yourself bonding with a friend by talking about another one?
3. What kind of friendship would feel ideal to you?
4. What lessons of friendship, both positive and negative, did you learn growing up?
5. Where would you like God to take you on this journey of friendship? Ask big.

CHAPTER TWO: THE FACTS OF MY LIFE

1. Are there darker chapters in your childhood story that you are reluctant to explore?
2. What in your childhood environment could have set up unhealthy responses from you?
3. What is one of your earliest childhood memories and what message did it write on your heart?
4. How would you describe the difference between being transparent and being vulnerable in your own life?

5. Have you ever experienced that feeling of Plexiglass in relationships?

CHAPTER THREE: IT'S OKAY TO BE NEEDY

1. What would you long to experience in a community of believers?

2. Have you ever gone through a time in your life when you felt like you were being hit from all sides? In hindsight, what do you think the purpose of that stormy season was?

3. How does the thought of being needy feel to you?

4. Can you identify with the illustration of a wall of self-protection built around your heart? Why do you think it is there?

5. What busyness is preventing you from having the time to invest in intimate relationships?

CHAPTER FOUR: A MERCIFUL BREAKDOWN

1. What are some so-called acceptable addictions you have turned to over the years?

2. Do you have a secret that you've never voiced to another person?

3. How does the thought of sharing in a group setting feel to you?

4. Were there any of the signs of codependency in friendships that sounded familiar to you? Which ones and how so?

5. Have you ever experienced the loss of a close friend? Did you allow yourself to fully grieve? How so? If not, where have you put the pain?

CHAPTER FIVE: WHERE DO I BEGIN?

1. What are your thoughts and feelings about intimate friendships with the opposite sex?
2. With which member of the Trinity do you relate more easily: God the Father, Jesus the Son, or the Holy Spirit?
3. Are there areas of your life where you feel as if you are walking in the dark?
4. If you could pray for sight, what would you ask for specifically?

CHAPTER SIX: NEW FRIENDSHIPS WITH OLD FRIENDS

1. Are there friends you've known for a long time with whom you'd like to go deeper? What can you do to initiate this new level of vulnerability?
2. What are three questions you can ask or conversation prompts you can use to deepen talks with friends the next time you gather?
3. Think of your own circle of relationships. What can you call out and appreciate in each person?
4. Who in your life would you describe as your closest friends, really close friends, and just friend-friends?

5. How can you more intentionally keep in touch with your close friends in the midst of your busy life?

CHAPTER SEVEN: WOMEN OF FAITH

1. Is there an area of your life where you know Satan is trying to discourage you? How can you fight him and the discouragement?

2. Do you have an "Emmitt"? If so, tell what you love most about her; if not, pray and ask for your "Emmitt" right now.

3. What does it mean to you to receive someone?

4. Think of your friendships. Is there healthy reciprocity in most of them?

5. Which friend might you write to on a regular basis—someone who could also double as a journaling partner?

CHAPTER EIGHT: WHO ARE SAFE PEOPLE?

1. Have you ever been betrayed by a friend? Have you been able to trust again?

2. Who would you like to be able to forgive—if you knew that you didn't have to forget and that it would take time for this person to earn your trust again?

3. What are some warning signs you've learned to pay attention to before giving your heart and trust to someone?

4. Think about friends whose words you hear but

whose actions you maybe ignore. What real message have you missed about your relationship?

5. How is your thinking distorted based on childhood experiences, and what might these distortions look like in your friendships?

CHAPTER NINE: AFRAID TO BE FREE

1. Are you more comfortable with rules or freedom? How so and why?

2. Does the idea of loosening the grip on Law and falling into grace sound exhilarating or frightening to you?

3. Do you think God will catch you if you let go of clinging to Law rather than to grace?

4. What person do you feel safe enough with to bring into the light a secret sin? Where and with whom are you that kind of person?

CHAPTER TEN: LET'S GET REAL

1. What might cause you to be hesitant to explore open, authentic friendships?

2. Think through your friends. Who feels real? Who feels safe?

3. How does the thought feel of inviting someone into your messy house or going out without makeup to meet them?

4. What response from a friend would you most desire after confessing your less-perfect side?

5. What do you usually do with your feelings? Express them or stuff them or something else?

Chapter Eleven: Conflict Can Be a Good Thing

1. Do you lean more toward being a people pleaser, a no-needer, or queen of everything?
2. Can you think of a brick in any of your current relationships that could morph into a wall? How can you tend to the issue that might block a friendship?
3. Have there been times in your relationships when you felt strong emotions about an issue that turned out to be merely an imagination balloon? How can you dare to pop such an imagining if one bounces up again?
4. To you, what is the goal of conflict resolution?

Chapter Twelve: From Head to Heart

1. How can you tell when a friend is really there, really present, with you?
2. What keeps you from reaching out and asking a friend for help?
3. Do you ever find yourself performing to earn or keep someone's love? When and how so?
4. What do you think God would say to you in the middle of a struggle with sin?
5. Which aspect of friendship discussed in this book has been most helpful to you?

Appendix One

You Gave Me a Friend

Sometimes we need help articulating our longings and desires. Allow me to share a prose poem I wrote and maybe it will help you put words to some of your desires for friendship.

Thank You, Lord, for this husband of mine.

We are growing old together, and he gets sexier with each curly gray hair. His gentle love heals my daddy-wounds. This one-flesh thing transcends his touch and mates my soul to his. Was I a computer geek before I met him? Is there any more peaceful place than lying snuggled within his spoon as I drift off into lesser dreams?

But he's a man, a good man, but just a man. And I'm a girl, a woman, with a little girl's heart. I need to giggle and be silly and, when my feelings get hurt, to cry. Other times, I don't know what I'm going to do about this matter or that, or what I think; I have to feel it, and I don't even know how I feel about it. There are rooms of my feminine soul where a man wouldn't want to go. But I don't want to be alone there. When my husband's patience has grown thin and his ears are full of my waxing philosophical and still I have leftover words . . .

You gave me a friend.

We can talk about the same four subjects from fifteen different angles and then question every conclusion and start all over again. My friend fills the emotional gaps left by a brilliantly analytical man. She knows how to listen with her eyes and talk with her heart. The oneness was there from the start because you have knit our hearts together, a tapestry of friendship.

Thank You, Holy Spirit, for the breath and life of my kids.

Flesh of my flesh, bone of my bone, heart of my heart. Somehow, the more I love from a reservoir I never knew I had, the greater my capacity to hold even more . . . to hold ever closer. Each child is nuzzled up within my soul, and I will nestle in theirs as they cuddle my grandchildren. With them I pray severely, hurt profoundly, love sprawlingly, and exhale thanks with every waking breath. My days are filled pouring out my life for them.

But they are children, precious gifts, for sure, but still little ones. And I am a little one too. Looking for one to care for me . . . care about me. Be my number one cheerleader. Ask me how I'm feeling and really care and then surprise me with a card or, better yet, candy . . . chocolate candy . . . dark chocolate candy . . . with nuts and chews . . . because she knows my favorites. When I'm tired of being tired and all "give out" . . . I exhale again that I'm so thankful . . .

You gave me a friend.

She gets down on her knees and helps me clean up the messes I alone have made. She has both eyes closed but both ears open if I call in the night. And somehow she always knows how to turn on the Light when I'm afraid of the dark. If I act like an insecure, immature child, she simply smiles and loves me anyway. I can be a whiny baby, and she will mother me and hold my heart until the hurt is all cried out. When I fall down, she picks me up and breathes refreshing words on my skinned needs.

Sweet Jesus, thank you for a gaggle of girlfriends.

Fun. Chocolate. Shopping. Coffee. "Just called to say, 'hi.'" Someone to go on a diet with and then go off with in the same day. Nothing blesses me more than knowing her kids are as bad as mine and her floors are stickier. A million recipes traded, cookies exchanged, in-home parties attended, casseroles delivered, kids babysat, husbands complained about, conversations interrupted, and laughter shared.

But they are just girlfriends, delightful every one, but all together not enough. In the deepest places only One can fit. In that tiny space, I keep my unspoken fears, shameful failures, the need to be needed, the want to be wanted, to know and be known. Just when I was afraid I wanted too much, asked too often, loved too big . . .

You gave me a friend.

A bucket to a hundred thimbles. Able to contain my overflow, no matter how much I gush . . . with room for more. Her capacity to receive is exceeded only by her capacity to give. I believe her when she reassures me that there is no such thing as loving too much. I feel safe. Safe enough to be seen by her without self-protection. She stands beside me, close enough for the salt from my tears to sting her own wounds. Yet she doesn't wince and run. She remains and allows my pain to cleanse hers too. She sees me. Really sees me. Into-Me-See . . . Intimacy.

Thank You, Heavenly Father, for the gift of Your Son.

There are no words. I have tried to express my love, but words fail me. It is like trying to build the Eiffel Tower with toothpicks. Descriptions of the gratitude I feel seem flimsy, miniature, reproduction. No lowercase word will ever define the uppercase Word. But I try nonetheless. I know you know, Lord. Even as a tiny ten-year-old girl, I wrote a school report on my best friend . . . it was you. It has been you all my life. My BFF, my Best Friend Forever . . . and eternal.

But you are up there . . . or in here . . . or everywhere at once . . . but someplace I can't see you or touch you or hear you. I want to look into your eyes and see myself . . . my true self. I want a hug, a real one, one I can really feel. I want to audibly hear the words "I love you," not just sense them or know them. The reality is you are infinite, beyond words, but I am not. I am finite, and I need words. Mercifully, You heard mine when I asked, and . . .

You gave me a friend.

A visible demonstration, physical manifestation, tangible incarnation of your love! Oh, thank you! Thank you for sending your Spirit to be with us, and thank you for sending your beloved daughter to be . . . with . . . me. Thank you for sending your Spirit to "come alongside" and thank you for sending my dearest friend to walk this journey beside me. Thank you that it is "I in you and you in me," and thank you that I can experience the connection I crave here on earth. This friendship is truly Heaven on Earth. Greater love has no man than this . . . First, you gave your life. And then you gave me a friend . . . for life.

Appendix Two

Practical Steps for Developing and Growing Friendships

I know that I sometimes read a book and think, *Okay, I know what to do, but I have no idea how to do it.* It is my hope that God has spoken to you through my personal story and that he is already speaking to your heart about specific steps toward more intimate friendships. At the same time, sometimes we need a friend to take our hand and walk beside us step-by-step to get started on our journey. With that in mind, I've created an appendix in more of a "how-to" format. I hope that it is a helpful reference for you as you take baby steps toward mature friendships.

CHAPTER ONE: I NEED FRIENDS

- Come up with some responses ahead of time to say when a friend starts talking negatively about another friend. Example: "Yes, I did notice that about her. I am so grateful for the mercy of God and my friends who love me even when I'm not perfect, either." Or: "I'd like to give her the benefit of the doubt; maybe there is another reason behind her behavior we just can't see."

- If you need someone to talk to and you don't have a safe friend, consider finding a counselor or pastor whom you can trust enough to share some of your secrets and fears and hurts.

- Make a list of your old friends. Take a risk and make the effort to contact them and perhaps rekindle a wonderful friendship from the past.

- Take a minute and remember that Jesus is the most perfect friend you can imagine. Now, pour out your heart to him, as if he were sitting across the table from you. Tell him where you are in your heart and what you're longing for.

CHAPTER TWO: THE FACTS OF MY LIFE

- Think of the wisest woman you know. Make an appointment with her to have coffee or tea and talk. Make a list of questions to ask her or topics to discuss.

- Think about your childhood. What are your earliest memories? Now, think about your whole life. What are some of the "messages" you may have written on your heart during a time of heightened or deepened emotion? Write these messages down. Are they Truth? If not, what would God have said to you in the middle of those memories?

- Contact three friends and invite them over for lunch and to play a game or talk.
- I wrote a book entitled, *Taking Care of the Me in Mommy.* I observed that moms (most women, for that matter) give and give and give, but if we don't take time to receive then we burn out. Friendships are refreshing for many women. Give yourself permission to invest in yourself by investing time in developing and sustaining friendships. Ultimately, you will have more to give to your family and work because you will give out of the overflow, rather than the dregs. Ironically, it is when we are the busiest that we need friends the most. Don't let busyness or "taking care of others" or too much responsibility keep you from tapping into the life source of friendships.

Chapter Three: It's Okay to Be Needy

- Find a personalized gift to exchange with your circle of friends to remind you to pray about three specific things for one another for a set number of weeks. Then meet for lunch to talk about how God has chosen to answer those prayers.
- Find a church that is offering a Bible study class. Invite a friend to sign up with you.
- Invite a couple of friends on a weekend getaway. Mark the calendar in advance and start saving and planning.

▣ Set aside a day to talk in depth and pray with a handful of friends.

▣ Call a friend and share something you have been turning over and over in your mind, rather than remain isolated with your inner experiences.

▣ Take an overview of your life and find three responsibilities that you can eliminate in order to make room for developing friendships.

CHAPTER FOUR: A MERCIFUL BREAKDOWN

▣ Call a friend and set up lunch or dinner or coffee. Don't put it off or wait for the perfect opportunity.

▣ Dare to share a secret with a safe and trustworthy friend.

▣ Call three friends for a three-minute "touch base" conversation. (Don't talk longer.) Start the conversation with, "I only have a few minutes, but . . ."

▣ Or call a friend and say, "Hey, I just called to say hello and I've been thinking about you and I would love to get a date on the calendar to meet you for a longer 'catch-up' talk."

▣ Eat a piece of chocolate and/or listen to a song with a friend. Pay attention and be aware of every sensation or emotion. Share your observations and reflections with each other.

▣ Go through the codependency checklist in this chapter and see if you can identify similar traits in yourself. If so, read a book about it.

- Join a group. You will find many different kinds:
  divorce, grief, addiction, codependency, adult children
  of alcoholics, sexual abuse, and eating disorders. I am
  currently in a group that is simply made up of women
  wanting deeper healing and emotional wholeness.
- Have an honest but probably difficult conversation
  with a friend about something that has been
  weighing on your heart and mind regarding the
  friendship.
- Bring your friendships before the Lord and ask if
  there are any relationships that aren't healthy for you.
  Sometimes the honest and best thing to do is to end a
  friendship. If someone needs more than you have to
  give and the relationship is draining you beyond what
  you have to offer, take care of yourself and trust God
  with the other person.
- If you have needed to end a friendship, or perhaps
  you are the one who has been "let go," give yourself
  permission and time to grieve the loss of what was
  good in the relationship.
- Think back over your life. Has there ever been a time
  when you lost someone or something but didn't allow
  yourself the freedom to fully grieve it all the way
  through? The hurt is still buried deep within your
  soul until you let it out. Find a friend with whom to
  talk it through, or cry with, or vent your confusion and
  anger with. Maybe you could write a letter to God and

read it aloud to him. As my friend Marilyn Meburg says, "You have to feel it to heal it."

- Do you know someone who is going through a hard time? Take a moment to send a card or a bar of chocolate or an uplifting CD. If you have time, put together a "box of comfort" with things you know would lift her spirits or warm her broken heart.

- If someone you know is in the middle of a trial or crisis or heartache, call her every day for a period of time just to let her know you are there. Give assurance that there is no need to respond, you just wanted to reach out and give a hug over the phone or by e-mail.

- Maybe you could call this friend every morning at the height of the crisis and say a quick prayer over her or send a prayer by e-mail every night so she can find comfort throughout the next day. (You may want to just call a friend and pray over her day regardless of whether she is in an obviously difficult time.)

- Give your friend all the time she needs to process her emotions: grief, anger, confusion, and sadness. Ask her if she'd like to talk about it and then just listen. Give her an opportunity to talk about the person or dream she lost.

- If you don't know what to say or do, be honest and say, "How can I be the best friend for you during this time? What do you want or need from me?"

- Look for tangible ways to love your friend during tough seasons. Pick up her laundry and return it washed, dried, and folded. Borrow her car and fill it up with gas and have it washed. Offer to keep her kids overnight. Think about what would bless you and do that for her.

Chapter Five: Where Do I Begin?

- Do you know someone who has gone through an experience similar to yours? Ask this person to consider being your "sponsor." Call this person when you need to talk about something rather than turning to less healthy ways of dealing with negative emotions.

- When you experience a current distressing feeling, ask yourself, "When have I felt this before . . ." Chances are, the hurt you are feeling today feels out of proportion to the current situation. That may be because it is tapping into deeper, past hurts. Deal with and process the original hurt, and it won't be as likely to resurface as often in your current friendships.

- When you experience an emotion, ask yourself "What is this emotion trying to tell me about something that needs attention under the hood?" Example: you feel compelled to turn to food or alcohol or shopping when deep down you know that you are attempting to feed or numb or distract from a deeper hurt.

- Think about and assess any friendships you might have with a man. In your heart of hearts, you will know whether you are "playing with fire" or whether this is a safe friendship. Take time to honestly think about this. If there is cause for concern, then talk about it with a friend, especially if you are ambivalent about ending the relationship.

◘ Find a friend who is in the same situation you are (for example: homeschool mom, pastor's wife, mom to a special needs child, single mom, a person struggling with weight, and so forth). Reach out to her to see if there could be a friendship there.

◘ The next time you experience something worth writing down, send it to a friend in an e-mail and then also save it in a "journal" file on your computer.

◘ Be intentional about making new friends. That seems so simple, but it may be the most practical tip in this appendix. If you don't make developing and sustaining friendships a priority, they won't happen.

◘ When looking for new friendship possibilities, nothing is more welcoming than a sincere warm smile with eye contact. Practice this. Bestselling author Andy Andrews says, "Smile when you talk!"

◘ Remember that timing is important when making new friends and for taking steps toward closer friendships. Pay attention to a patient pace.

◘ Take the risk to reach out, knowing that you may get hurt or be rejected. Realize that not everyone desires to add friends into their lives at this time. Don't take this personally. Keep reaching out.

- Keep an open heart and an open mind. Look for friends who are different from you in background, race, socioeconomic status, faith, politics, or stage of life. Purposely foster a friendship with someone whom others might reject for one reason or another.
- Be the social coordinator. Take the initiative. Plan an event. Put something together. Step out. Be the leader.
- Maybe you could start a "MomTime" group. Refer to my book *How to Start Your Own MomTime* from Focus on the Family.
- Plan a Bunco party. (Look on the Internet for rules and instructions.)
- Christmas is a good time to meet your neighbors. Host an Open House. Organize a Christmas Coffee. (See www.womentoday.org/Christmas.htm.) Host an after-Christmas party and exchange gifts that you've bought on sale.
- What do you love to do? Cook? Paint? Sew? Scrapbook? Exercise? Shop at a consignment shop? Track down garage sales? Either find a friend to join you or use your gifts to bless a friend with what you've created or found.
- Set a weekly or monthly time on the calendar to call a friend. Maybe Saturday mornings while the kids watch cartoons or Wednesday night after the kids are in bed or Tuesday mornings when they are at school. The key is consistency and intentionality.

Chapter Six: New Friendships with Old Friends

- Ask a couple of friends to write an e-mail to you describing how they experience you. This might feel embarrassing, but your friends will probably enjoy this, and it will encourage you. While writing this book, I asked some friends to do this for me. Their words were treasures I will keep in my heart forever. They also encouraged me that I was farther along the friend road than I thought I was. I needed that affirmation to keep going.

- Think of a handful of friends and then write down what each of their particular personalities or lives has taught you or how it has blessed you. Send it to them, maybe in a pretty note card.

- Drive to see an old friend or reconnect with a childhood buddy.

- Dare to share a doubt or a question about life you have with an old friend.

- The next time someone calls to connect with you, unless it is simply not possible, try to make time for this.

- Make a list of your three really close friends and twelve close friends. Don't attempt to have twelve really close friends. It really isn't possible, and it will only frustrate you and them.

- Keep in touch with old friends. Facebook is a great way to do this.

- Create a "Milestones" calendar. Fill in the dates with

your friends' birthdays and anniversaries but don't overlook other important dates. I once sent a balloon bouquet on a friend's one-year-sober birthday. I sent flowers to a friend on the date of her child's death. The day a friend's divorce is final is often a very lonely day. Make notes of special or difficult dates, and let your friend know that you haven't forgotten by sending a note or e-mail on that day. You can also set up reminders on your computer calendar for upcoming special dates.

◫ Create a Happy Birthday or Just Thinking of You e-mail template and save it as a file on your computer. Now, all you need to do is insert your friend's name with a personal greeting and hit the "Send" button. (You may want to change it each January 1.)

◫ Keep a box of assorted occasions and blank cards on hand.

◫ Do a project with a friend: paint a room, rake the leaves, go on a mission trip, visit a homeless shelter, or run/walk in a 10k race, like one for breast cancer awareness.

◫ Join something together: choir, evening college class, craft lessons, cooking lessons.

◫ There is nothing like just taking time to send an old-fashioned handwritten note to a friend for no particular reason. My friend Bridget is a master at this. I don't think she has any idea how often she touches hearts at just the right time.

- Pay attention when you start thinking of a friend out of the blue. It could be God prompting you to reach out.
- Work at being a good friend. Learn about friends—it is worth the effort. Ask them to share their photo albums or favorite books, movies, or music.
- Take a personality test together. (You can find them online.) Learn each other's love languages. (See *The 5 Love Languages* by Gary Chapman, Northfield Publishing.) Take Marcus Buckingham's Strong Life Test for Women, *www.stronglifetest.com*. Now talk about how you can be more understanding friends.

CHAPTER SEVEN: WOMEN OF FAITH

- Make plans to attend a Women of Faith event (find out details at www.womenoffaith.com) and invite a friend. Better yet, gather a group of friends and become a group leader.
- Consider being a mentor to someone younger than you. Reach out, invite her to join you for coffee, and encourage her to ask you questions or share her heart.
- Write to a friend tonight and tell her all about your day. Invite her to do the same if she has time. Be intentional about receiving her e-mail by replying back with comments to things she has shared about her day.
- Start an ongoing e-mail exchange with a friend. Begin with, "Today I am grateful for . . ." Send one sentence and invite your friend to return the e-mail with her

gratitude sentence. Keep this up daily. It is a great way
to keep an attitude of gratitude while also learning
about your friend.

- Start a Circle of Friends journal. Buy a blank journal
  and write in it for a week. Then send it to a friend and
  ask her to do the same. Then she can send it to the
  next friend. Keep the circle to no more than four
  friends. Each person has a week to record her
  thoughts and feelings, and then you get the gift of
  seeing inside the heart and lives of three other friends.
- Pray and ask God to show you how you can be a
  better friend to someone in particular.
- Send a random text message to a friend telling her
  how grateful you are for her and why.
- Become a "Secret Pal." For a month, send encouraging
  cards without signing the cards. Or leave a little gift in her
  mailbox or on her doorstep. Encourage her to simply
  practice receiving without any way of returning the favor.
  This is a fun way to give and receive unconditional love.
- Reach out and ask someone to pray for you.
- Pray about it, and then find a friend with whom you
  can commit to meeting intentionally on a weekly basis.
- Read a book with a friend and then trade books so you
  can read each other's highlighted notes. Get together
  and talk about what touched you or taught you.
- Be intentional about growing closer to a particular
  friend.

▣ Next time you are together, ask the question, "How are you in your soul?"

▣ Be a sleuth. Notice what your friend likes and dislikes. What she wants and needs. What she loved growing up. Her favorites: coffee drink, candy, musician, author, and so on.

▣ Use eBay in a fun way to surprise a friend. For example, I recently bought two mugs for a friend. One had Anderson Cooper's picture on it, and the other one was from Ben & Jerry's Ice Cream factory—two of her favorites! She responded with my favorite thank-you note ever: "Far surpassing any tangible gift you gave, is the enormous gift that you *knew* me . . . knew what would be meaningful to me. For that I thank you beyond measure."

CHAPTER EIGHT: WHO ARE SAFE PEOPLE?

▣ Think through your friends: identify the ones who gossip or talk about other people. Now, think through your friends and take note of the ones who speak positively about others. Also, be on the lookout for "perfect people." Be careful about being too vulnerable with them. They may not understand or be able to tolerate imperfection.

▣ Observe the fruit of a person's life over time before allowing her into your heart.

▣ Give friendships time; don't go too deep too fast. Take

time to tiptoe into deeper conversation and more intimate areas of disclosure.

- Learn and rehearse a phrase for when someone asks a question that feels too invasive. Something like, "I appreciate that you want to know me better, but I just don't feel comfortable sharing that yet."

- Write a note forgiving a friend, but first tell God exactly how you feel about the situation.

- If you are the person receiving forgiveness, then receive it fully. Trust that you are forgiven and try not to act awkward or ashamed. Start over with a clean slate.

- Illustrate your emotional bank account. Where are the areas and who are the people withdrawing from your reserves? Now, from which sources are you being replenished? Is your emotional bank account balanced? If not, consider making some "budget cuts" or investing more time in areas or people where there is the highest return.

- Identify "buckets, cups, and thimbles" in your friendships. This exercise is not to stand in judgment—there are very understandable reasons why some people do not have the time or capacity to offer much. But it is good to take an honest, realistic survey so that you don't expect more than is possible and then set your friendship up for disappointment.

- Pay attention to what someone does, not just what she says. For instance, if a friend says, "Call me," and when you do she is never available, you may want to wait for her to reach out the next time.

- On the other hand, be honest and up-front with what you offer of yourself. Ney has taught me to start with a "receiving statement" like, "Thank you so much for inviting me to____ (*fill in the blank*). Unfortunately, my calendar is full, and I know myself well enough to know that I must also schedule in plenty of downtime. I better not overcommit myself. But, it means a lot to me that you would think of me."

- The next time a friend confesses a weakness or fear or mistake to you, don't give a scripture or advice. Find a way to empathize. If she asks for your opinion, then gladly share from your experience if a Bible verse or solution has helped you. If you haven't been through a similar experience, consider reminding her how big God is or how much he loves her.

- Are you taking on too much responsibility for a friend? Consider reading *Boundaries* by Henry Cloud and John Townsend and *Changes That Heal* by Henry Cloud if you desire emotional healing and growth.

CHAPTER NINE: AFRAID TO BE FREE

- We have seasons in friendships. Staying connected through different seasons of friendships often requires grace and understanding.

- One of the more difficult seasons to weather is when one or both of you have small children. It is very difficult to find extra time to nurture relationships outside of the family. Here are a few practical tips that might help a little. (There is also an entire chapter on friends in my book *Taking Care of the Me in Mommy* with many more suggestions.)

- Multitask by using a cordless headset phone to talk to a friend who is doing the same while washing dishes, sorting laundry, or doing other household chores.

- Whenever you find yourself waiting in a bank line or car pool line, send a quick "Thinking of you in the midst of our busy lives" text.

- Keep a speed dial list of your friends in your cell phone. The next time you find yourself with a minute of alone time, call up a friend for a quick chat.

- Wait until the kids are in bed and dad is watching a favorite show. Steal away to your local Starbucks or bookstore for a cup of decaf and close conversation with a friend.

- Find opportunities to spend time with your friend while also including the husbands and children: park play dates, Saturday afternoon community pool and BBQ, spaghetti dinner and DVD night.

- Invite friends to join you on an errand you both need to do: grocery store, Target, gym, and so forth.

- Take a "virtual" shopping trip with a friend. Take

advantage of your cell phone camera and snap pictures of cute shoes you see, a yummy piece of chocolate cake you are eating, or a smile-producing item you discover and send the picture to your friend right then.

◘ Download and send a song that will inspire a friend or say what you are feeling or what you'd like to say.

◘ Check into using Skype to video chat with a friend from your home.

◘ Sign up for my free "Personal Mom Coaching" (www. LisaWhelchel.com) service from my Web site and allow me to be a virtual friend.

◘ During lean financial seasons of life, make an extra casserole for a friend or shop warehouse clubs together.

◘ Can't afford to meet out for coffee or lunch? Invite a friend over to your house for a donut and coffee or chips and a soda.

◘ Take advantage of online greeting cards to stay in touch with friends and remember them on their special days.

Chapter Ten: Let's Get Real

◘ Invite a safe friend to join you in an authentic friendship.

◘ Choose a safe person and tell her how you are really feeling, the way it really is, who you really are.

◘ Be up-front about what you are wanting/needing in a friendship.

- Tell a friend if you are in trouble: financially, in your marriage, spiritually, or with your children.

- Ask a friend the question, "Where are you emotionally right now?" Concentrate on listening without feeling the need to respond. Simply say, "Thank you for trusting me enough to share your heart with me. It is a privilege."

- Ask your friend how you can pray for her. This shows you care. Then you can give the priceless gift of prayer. Write a prayer and send it in a note or an e-mail.

- Some people just don't prefer intimate conversation or conflict resolution. If the friendship is worth it, press in but don't push.

- Some people won't open up unless you ask. If you discern a concern, gently ask but give grace if she is not ready to share. Remind your friend that you really want to know how she is feeling. It isn't a burden or a rote question. Some people need convincing of your interest because of past hurts and disappointments.

- If someone has shared something personal with you, ask her about it at a later time. She will know that you paid attention, valued her feelings, and still care how she is.

- Most importantly, listen, listen, listen. When it is time to respond, speak from your heart first and then from your head.

- The other day, I let out a heavy sigh. My friend

Marilyn immediately said, "Put words to that sigh and share with me what you are feeling." I loved that.

◘ Ask a friend the three questions Jennifer and I asked in this chapter: 1. "What do you see in my life that encourages you?" 2. "What do you see in my life that you would caution me about?" 3. "What else would you like to say?"

◘ Ask a friend the two questions I asked Marilyn: 1. "What do I do that draws me to you?" 2. "What do I do that pushes you away?"

◘ As a fun getting-to-know-you game, gather a few friends and write on a piece of paper two true things about you and one lie. Have them guess which one is the lie. This makes for enlightening conversation and surprising self-disclosure.

Chapter Eleven: Conflict Can Be a Good Thing

◘ The pastor of my church has a wonderful phrase he repeats often, "Change leads to conflict, which leads to growth. This is the cycle of success." This is also true of successful friendships.

◘ If you are experiencing conflict with a friend, the first thing to do is pray. Nothing breaks down barriers faster. Next, give each other the benefit of the doubt. Don't discuss your feelings with everyone else first. Go directly to your friend. Try to resolve conflict as soon as possible. It is too easy for it to fester or "go under" only to pop up later disguised and more difficult to unmask.

▣ Are there any unspoken bad feelings or miscommunications that could benefit from a "brick at a time" conversation? Granted, not everything warrants bringing up for discussion since love does cover a multitude of sins. Only you can determine whether leaving it unvoiced could create a wedge between you. For instance, I have a friend who is always late. This doesn't bother me. I understand that she has three small children, and it is difficult to get out the door on time. So, I've learned to pack a book to read while I wait. On the other hand, I have another friend who takes it as a personal affront if I am late to meet her. I am grateful that she took the time to explain to me that her time is valuable and that when I cancel at the last minute or am late to meet her, it feels like I am not respecting her schedule.

▣ The next time you realize you are having an imaginary dialogue in your head about how you think a friend is feeling, invite her into the dialogue and allow her to speak for herself. You may just need to pop an imagination balloon.

▣ Are you experiencing a disagreement or misunderstanding with a friend? Have a "Pepsi Can" conversation and share each of your perspectives. Work to understand her point of view and come together with a win/win solution.

- If you are having a difficult conversation with a friend, strive to listen with your heart, not just hear her words. She may be angry because she feels so invested in this friendship or because you have touched a deep hurt from her past.
- In any conflict, ask God to show you what you can learn. Even if you determine that only one percent of the problem is you, own that and apologize. This creates an atmosphere of openness and reconciliation.

Chapter Twelve: From Head to Heart

- Practice being present with a friend. Stop everything and be there. Put your cell phone on vibrate. If possible, don't multitask, even if you feel like you can do something else and listen at the same time. Let her know that you are there by your body language and eye contact. Ask follow-up questions.
- Practice being present with yourself. When possible, drive in the car without the radio on. Sit still without reading or watching television. Start small, but become comfortable with longer periods of silence and solitude.
- Practice being present with God. Pour out your heart but then take time to listen. Or simply imagine you are leaning up against Jesus like his disciple John (John 13:25). Breathe out your worries and breathe in his peace.
- Imagine yourself stepping to the throne of grace with

all your feelings of shame and unworthiness. Now, picture him smiling and delighting in you because you are his beloved daughter.

- Call someone just to talk through your feelings.
- Call someone and ask for specific prayer.
- When people ask you to pray for them, offer to pray with them right then.
- Send a card, text, or e-mail that says, "I have prayed for you." That is so much more comforting than, "I will pray for you."
- Collect your friends' Christmas card photos and put them on the fridge or a bulletin board nearby. Whenever your eyes land upon a family, send up a quick prayer for them.
- If a sermon touches you at church, buy the CD and send it to a friend. If a book helps you grow, buy one for a friend. (Maybe this one. ☺)
- Send a box of "withness" to a friend. Collect a handful of little gifts, wrap them individually, put a sweet note on each package, box them all up, and deliver it to a friend who needs a friend to be with her during a lonely or hard time.
- Consider attempting to reconcile a broken friendship.
- Think of the kind of friendships you would like to have and ask God to provide that kind of friend.

Appendix Three

Conversation Prompts

O ne of my very favorite things to do with my friends is ask questions. Here are random questions I have asked over the years. Typically, you won't need to ask more than two or three because they have the capacity to open up conversation that can last for hours. Start with a question and then allow the conversation to go where it wants to go. Follow its lead and discover the thrill of intimate friendship.

- What do people say you do best?
- Describe an ideal day for you.
- What, if anything, would you like to be different in your life?
- What do you hope your life will look like in one to five years?
- Tell me a couple of high points and a couple of challenges in your day/week/month.
- I'd love to hear your story. Start from the beginning and don't leave anything out.
- Describe some key relationships in your life. How have these influenced you?

- Describe where you are in your heart/life in three words.
- If you could go to Disney World with any celebrity alive today, who would it be?
- What's your favorite breakfast food?
- If you could have a super power, what would it be? And, who is your favorite superhero?
- What is your favorite childhood memory?
- What is your favorite Bible verse? What's your favorite proverb? What's your favorite psalm?
- When you get to heaven, what is the first thing you're going to say to God?
- What is something you've done that has been over the top?
- If you could have dinner with anyone from the Bible, who would it be and why?
- Tell me about your first kiss. Or your first date.
- If you were an animal, what would you be?
- What quality do you admire most in another individual?
- What do you value most in a friendship?
- What is the hardest commandment to keep?
- What did I not ask you that you wish I had?
- What is your favorite nursery rhyme?
- Who was your favorite childhood TV star?
- What is your dream of happiness?
- What's the one sound that drives you crazy?
- What is the first job you ever had?
- What is one thing you wouldn't want to live without?
- If you could have any animal in the world as a pet, what would that be?

- If you were going to be in the Olympics, in what sport would you compete?
- Who was your first celebrity crush?
- What is your favorite book?
- What do you like to do on a rainy day?
- What movie could you watch over and over again?
- If you could change something about yourself, what would it be?
- What profession other than your own would you like to attempt?
- What is your favorite smell?
- Who is your favorite actor/actress? Why?
- What is your favorite thing to do?
- If you could only subscribe to one magazine for the rest of your life, what would it be?
- If you were a vegetable/fruit, what kind would you be?
- Who is considered to be your hero?
- How do you relieve stress?
- What quality do you most admire in a man?
- Do you have a motto?
- If you could play any musical instrument, what would it be?
- What is the best advice anyone has given you?
- What is your favorite place in the world?
- What is your favorite guilty pleasure?
- What do you think people remember most about you?
- What do you often daydream about?
- What in nature do you find most beautiful?
- What scares you the most and why?
- Who is your favorite Disney character?

- What would you attempt if you could not fail?
- What is your favorite song on your iPod?
- What is your favorite food?
- If you could be someone else for a day, who would it be?
- Do you remember your favorite teacher?
- Do you have any bad habits?
- What is your first thought when you wake up in the morning? What is your last thought before you go to bed?
- Do you have any hidden talents?
- If the whole world were listening, what would you say?
- What is the best song to describe your life?
- What is your favorite holiday?
- What is one thing you love about being an adult?
- What is one thing you miss about being a child?
- What is the best band of all time?
- Where did you take your last vacation?
- When you were a child, what did you want to be when you grew up?
- When people look back on your life, how do you want to be remembered?
- What sound or noise do you love?
- If you could have dinner with anyone, who would it be?
- What is your favorite wardrobe accessory?
- What is one thing about you that people would be surprised to find out?
- Who are your two most trusted friends? Why?
- If you could do anything at all and money were no problem, what would you love to do with your life?
- What's standing in the way of what you'd like to be or do?

- What keeps you up at night?
- How would your friends/loved ones describe you?
- How would your competitors or critics describe you?
- What do you hope to accomplish in the remainder of your life?
- What do you wish you had known or done ten years ago?
- How did you decide to _____?
- May I ask your advice about _____?
- What can I do to make your day?
- What do you need most right now?
- What concerns do you have?
- What emotion(s) are you least comfortable experiencing? (anger, anticipation, anxiety, boredom, confusion, disgust, fear, joy, love)
- When you feel these uncomfortable emotions, how do you respond? What do you feel, think, and say?
- What's your favorite Dr. Seuss book?
- If you could live in any home on a television series, what would it be?
- What's your favorite Web site?
- What's your favorite school supply?
- What's the best bargain you've ever found at a garage sale or thrift store?
- What's the most interesting biography you've read?
- What's your least favorite word? Your most favorite word?
- Describe something that's happened to you for which you have no explanation.
- What is the most incredible experience you've ever had with God or heard of someone else having?

- Was there ever a time in your life when you know that you would have died if not for the grace of God?
- If you could travel anywhere in the world, where would it be?
- Where do you go for advice?
- What's the sickest you've ever been?
- What's your favorite form of exercise?
- What's the biggest lesson I might be able to learn from you?
- What's the biggest lesson you think you can learn from me?

Notes

Chapter Two: The Facts of My Life

1. Henry Cloud and John Townsend, *How People Grow* (Grand Rapids: Zondervan, 2001, 2004), 233.

2. Henry Cloud, *Changes That Heal* (Grand Rapids: Zondervan, 1997), 95.

Chapter Three: It's Okay to Be Needy

1. Henry Cloud, *Changes That Heal* (Grand Rapids: Zondervan, 1997), 95.

2. Ibid.

3. Henry Cloud and John Townsend, *How People Grow* (Grand Rapids: Zondervan, 2001, 2004), 85.

4. Ibid., 123.

Chapter Four: A Merciful Breakdown

1. Henry Cloud and John Townsend, *How People Grow* (Grand Rapids: Zondervan, 2001, 2004), 265.

2. Walter Wangerin Jr., *Mourning into Dancing* (Grand Rapids: Zondervan, 1996), 96.

Chapter Five: Where Do I Begin?

1. Henri Nouwen, *The Inner Voice of Love* (New York: Doubleday Image, 1998, 1999), xiii.

2. Jennifer Rothschild, *Walking by Faith: Lessons Learned in the Dark* (Nashville: LifeWay, 2003 Bible Study Workbook Ed.), 16.

3. Ibid.

4. Ibid., 95.

5. Ibid., 63.

CHAPTER SEVEN: WOMEN OF FAITH

1. Edith Schaeffer, *L'Abri* (Wheaton, IL: Crossway, 1992), 53.

2. Henry Cloud and John Townsend, *12 "Christian" Beliefs That Can Drive You Crazy* (Grand Rapids: Zondervan, 1995), 128.

CHAPTER EIGHT: WHO ARE SAFE PEOPLE?

1. Henry Cloud, *Changes That Heal* (Grand Rapids: Zondervan, 1997), 96.

CHAPTER NINE: AFRAID TO BE FREE

1. Henri Nouwen, *Our Greatest Gift: A Meditation on Dying and Caring* (New York:HarperCollins, 1994), 63.

2. Richard Rohr, *The Naked Now* (Chestnut Ridge, NY: Crossroad Publishing Co., 2009), 80.

3. Joseph R. Cooke, *Celebration of Grace* (Grand Rapids: Zondervan, 1991), 13.

4. Rohr, 127.

5. Henry Cloud and John Townsend, *How People Grow* (Grand Rapids: Zondervan, 2001, 2004), 182.

CHAPTER TEN: LET'S GET REAL

1. Shauna Niequist, *Cold Tangerines* (Grand Rapids: Zondervan, 2007), 50.

2 Henry Cloud, "Blocks to Love," 2000, Cloud-Townsend Solutions for Life, http://www.cloudtownsend.com/library/articles/7articles1.php. Accessed February 6, 2010.

3. http://www.cloudtownsend.com.

CHAPTER ELEVEN: CONFLICT CAN BE A GOOD THING
   1. Ney Bailey, *Faith Is Not a Feeling* (Colorado Springs: WaterBrook Press, 1978, 1993, 2002), 62.

CHAPTER TWELVE: FROM HEAD TO HEART
   1. Henri Nouwen, *Out of Solitude* (Notre Dame: Ave Maria, 1974, 2004), 38.
   2. Henry Cloud and John Townsend, *12 "Christian" Beliefs That Can Drive You Crazy* (Grand Rapids: Zondervan, 1995), 127.

About the Author

$\mathcal{L}$isa Whelchel, whose first appearance on *The New Mickey Mouse Club* launched her busy acting career, is best known for her role as Blair on the perennial hit TV show *The Facts of Life*. She is the author of fifteen books, including *Creative Correction, The Facts of Life and Other Lessons My Father Taught Me, Taking Care of the Me in Mommy,* and *The ADVENTure of Christmas*. Lisa and her husband, Steve, live in Texas with their three children, Tucker, Haven, and Clancy.

Visit her Web site at www.lisawhelchel.com.